WALLABY

Annette Annechild's WOK YOUR WAY SKINNY! 30-DAY MENU PLAN

Illustrated by
Cristina Eisenberg

A WALLABY BOOK
Published by Simon & Schuster, Inc. • New York

Published by Wallaby Books
A Division of Simon & Schuster, Inc.
Simon & Schuster Building
1230 Avenue of the Americas
New York, New York 10020
Designed by Irving Perkins Associates
WALLABY and colophon are registered trademarks of Simon &
Schuster, Inc.
First Wallaby Books printing July, 1984
10 9 8 7 6 5 4 3 2 1
Manufactured in the United States of America
Printed and bound by Command Web
ISBN: 0-671-50034-1

Lovingly dedicated to the memory of those I cherish:

Charles McFall
Cathy Reagan Laks
Otto Anastasio
Lucia Anastasio
Fred Pelligrino
Jimmy Hayden
Marilyn Monroe
John Lennon
Elvis Presley
Rev. Swami Sivananda

With many thanks to these very special people:
Stanley Goodman • Lanell Doré • Christopher Brenner •
Susie Burgos • Ed and Eileen Friedman • Raymond
Heremaia • Lisa Stewart • Barry and Paula Hamilton • John
Boswell • Patti Brown • Melissa Newman • Gene Brissie •
Susan Bailey • Jack Artenstein • my illustrator Cristina
Eisenberg and her husband Stevie • Melodie Woods • Bob
Celecia • Debbie and Tony Viscardi • John Michael Kelly •
Annie Brody • Julius and Dina Lieberman • Bob, Barbara
and Leonora Tint • Cyd Smith • River • Jean and John
Holdamph • my parents Frank and Anne Viscardi • Mrs.
Gooch and her Produce Department • Joseph Plewa •
Richard Anteau • Carl Wilson • Richard Gunther • Patrick
Netter • Wende West • John Johnson • Regis Philbin • Gail
Bilco • Skip Skwarek • Claude Baruc • Stephane Kriegel •
Chad Hamrin • Leah Komaiko • Monica Harutuhian • Pusha
Cariolagian • Tom Atman Fronterhouse • Rev. Swami
Satchidananda—and to all my students and teachers. *Your
spirit touched here. . . .*

*Those who have health
have hope—and
Those who have hope
have everything—
Victory to that master
that lives inside each
one of us—Victory!*

—Daily Yogi Prayer

The Natural Order of Things

4

THE NATURAL KITCHEN 33

5

THE 30-DAY MENU PLAN 49

Annette Annechild's WOK YOUR WAY SKINNY!

30-DAY

MENU PLAN

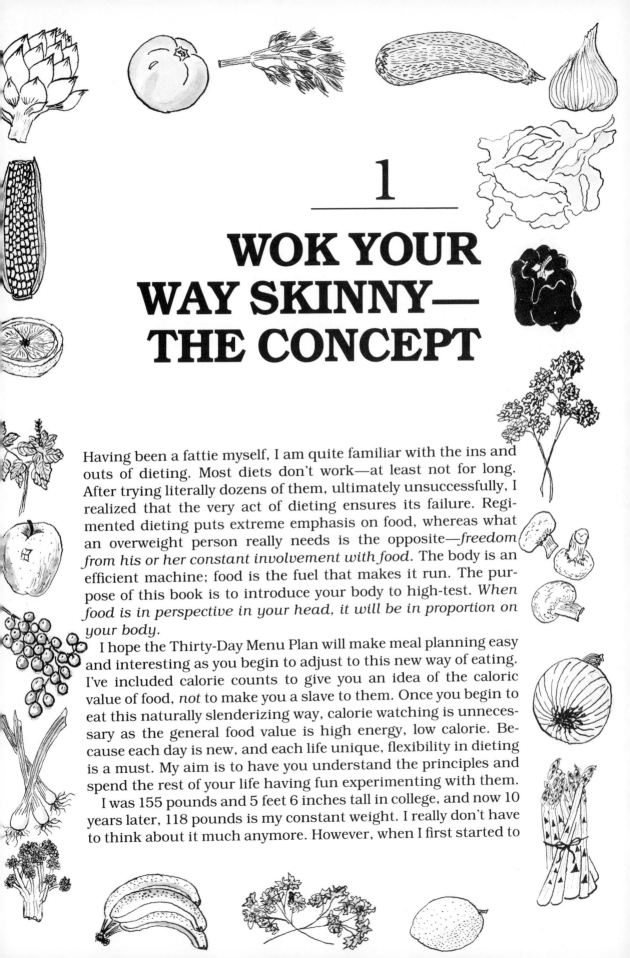

1

WOK YOUR WAY SKINNY— THE CONCEPT

Having been a fattie myself, I am quite familiar with the ins and outs of dieting. Most diets don't work—at least not for long. After trying literally dozens of them, ultimately unsuccessfully, I realized that the very act of dieting ensures its failure. Regimented dieting puts extreme emphasis on food, whereas what an overweight person really needs is the opposite—*freedom from his or her constant involvement with food*. The body is an efficient machine; food is the fuel that makes it run. The purpose of this book is to introduce your body to high-test. *When food is in perspective in your head, it will be in proportion on your body.*

I hope the Thirty-Day Menu Plan will make meal planning easy and interesting as you begin to adjust to this new way of eating. I've included calorie counts to give you an idea of the caloric value of food, *not* to make you a slave to them. Once you begin to eat this naturally slenderizing way, calorie watching is unnecessary as the general food value is high energy, low calorie. Because each day is new, and each life unique, flexibility in dieting is a must. My aim is to have you understand the principles and spend the rest of your life having fun experimenting with them.

I was 155 pounds and 5 feet 6 inches tall in college, and now 10 years later, 118 pounds is my constant weight. I really don't have to think about it much anymore. However, when I first started to travel frequently, my weight pushed right back up; it was that deadly American fare that did it. White bread, desserts, breaded fried foods—no wonder our nation is filled with fat people! *But you can be different.* You can have a sleek, beautiful body that is filled with vitality. It's back to the basics, back to the earth, back to wonderfully fresh whole foods, *welcome home. . . .*

Every Day

When you want to improve some aspect of yourself, the most important element for success is incorporating the new program into your daily routine. I've found this to be true with skin care, oral hygiene, exercise, and most certainly with food. A daily routine that includes time to care for oneself is essential—especially after age thirty. You just can't get away with what you did in your twenties. It's also never too late to start looking and feeling younger. Telling yourself "you have no time" is self-defeating. We all have the same twenty-four hours. We all have responsibilities. But I believe we also have a responsibility to care for ourselves. We must make time to care for our skin, teeth, and bodies, or we pay a high price. I have come to enjoy my daily routines of caring for myself, and the rewards are great. I look and feel my best and have the good feeling of being in control of my life in the most positive sense. I wasn't born a natural beauty—so few of us are. I've worked at being the best I can be and that in itself is a great reward. At thirty-two, I look a thousand times better than I did at eighteen. It just takes a little effort, a little time, and a lot of self-love!

Self-love

Food is a wonderful place to begin with the notion of self-love. We feed ourselves to watch ourselves grow. Food is the body's nourishment. When we abuse that principle and use food to combat emotional needs and stress, we begin to punish our bodies and the effects are staggering—bad skin, fat, low energy, nervousness, disease. *What goes into your mouth shows in your being.* If you want clear glowing skin, a lean body with strong, calm energy that is *dis-ease* free, come with me. Come and see how simple that really can be. It's habit, mostly, that has people eating so poorly. The habits of a country where food technology led us in a very wrong direction. Frozen, canned, processed, preserved—it sounded good, I guess, when it started. The attempt was to make food convenient; the results were deadly. Most of us have forgotten or have never experienced real food. Fresh vegetables, whole grains, fertile eggs, fresh fish—all so easy to prepare, so delicious to the taste, so economical in the budget. We are speaking here of things larger than a thirty-day diet. We are talking about what a human body needs to grow and flourish. If you come this way and rediscover real food, you will look and feel much differently than your fellow Americans. You will be thin, firm, and glowing with energy that is naturally high. We all must teach each other.

Fat Head

I've always believed that fat starts in the mind, not in the body. When you're trapped in fat, you don't need another calorie chart or carbohydrate counter. You need a whole new mental picture. So before we actually start using the wok, I thought it important to set some gentle mental guidelines for your journey into this world of natural, good eating. I've put together the mental guidelines that I feel are responsible for my being a person who is finally thin, who, after years of torment, can put on a pair of size-7 jeans with a sigh of happy disbelief that they fit beautifully. I love being thin, and I'm convinced that anyone can be there, too. No matter what anyone says, it does make an enormous difference in your life. So read the guidelines slowly, then go over them again. They can make the difference in your diet and your state of mind. When you're ready, read on; have fun learning about woks. New, natural ways of eating can take the emphasis off dieting, and that's very important. Pounds will slip away as you enjoy food more than ever.

The Gentle Mental Guidelines

1. Begin by starting to think of food as a friend, not as an evil tempter. Food is a primary source of nourishment to be carefully selected and slowly savored. A diet that will work forever must be based on respect and love for oneself—not deprivation and punishment.
2. Be aware of everything you put in your mouth. Ask yourself

if you really want it, is it good for you, and do you need to eat it *now*. Remember, you can always have it later or tomorrow or next week. (Food will not have disappeared off the face of the earth by tomorrow!)

3. Eat slowly and delicately, and take breaks during your meals to see if you are full. Start to listen to your stomach. It's on your side!

4. If you want a doughnut, eat a *doughnut*. Don't eat out half the refrigerator instead and still want the doughnut. Eat it, enjoy it, and forget about it.

5. Exercise is, of course, important. On days when you are too tired to *do* a lot, be too tired to *eat* a lot.

6. Chew your food extremely well. It makes all the difference. Essential enzymes are released as you masticate your food. Remember, digestion begins in the mouth. Thirty to fifty chews per mouthful is said to be ideal.

7. Eat when you're hungry, stop when you're full, and don't be afraid to miss a meal occasionally.

8. Never eat if you are angry, excited, upset, in a hurry, or planning to go to bed in the next two hours. It's terrible for you!

9. Don't feel you owe anything to anyone when it comes to food. It's your body. If you don't want something, don't eat it. Better to fast than feast in social situations where the food is not right for you.

10. Love yourself a *lot*, no matter what. You are what you've got this time around. Appreciate your progress and forgive your slipups. Each day you can begin again. . . .

Your Daily Diet

Every day it is important to have:

· plenty of fresh vegetables
· a whole grain
· a source of protein
· miso soup (both instant and an easy recipe on page 38 are available)
· beverages (should be selected from spring water, apple juice, herb tea)

Take in moderation:

Wine, light beer, honey, yogurt, cheese, eggs, milk, poultry, fish, whole-wheat bread, and pita pockets.

Avoid:

Cigarettes, coffee, pekoe tea, hard liquor, red meat, veal, pork, lamb, white bread and white-flour products, sugar, artificial sweeteners, soda and diet soda, nondairy creamers, preserved foods.

The benefits:

Better skin, better hair, better body—*better life*!

Now if all this seems too severe for you, remember any change is best made gradually. The 30-Day Plan will at least ensure that your meals are healthy and slimming. The rest you must deal with as well as you can. If you *must* have sugar or meat occasionally, have it. Understand the effects of such foods and watch for those effects. See how you *feel*; learn to listen to your body, it will tell you everything. If you stick to the diet, you will lose a great deal of weight and you will feel terrific. No more indigestion, no more self-hate the morning after. If you are now taking any drugs such as laxatives, antacids, etc., on a regular basis, the need for them will drift away. The body will begin to function as it was created to, and all those bottles will be junk on your shelves you can get rid of.

Grace

Before eating it is a good idea to pause for a moment. Roll your head around your shoulders, have a few long deep breaths, reflect for a moment—perhaps thanking the earth for her generous bounty. Never eat on the run. Sit up straight, chew well. After dining, a fifteen-minute period of relaxation is recommended.

Why This Diet Works So Quickly

The reason this diet works so well is that it is fat-free. *Fat makes fat.* Basically, you can eat as much as you need of fresh vegetables with lean meats such as fish or poultry taken in moderation. Grain has a cleansing effect. It absorbs the impurities in the body and provides the fiber to push them out of the system.

Also there is a minimum of dairy in this diet. Dairy forms mucus, it clogs the system, it gives a round padded look to the flesh. In case of a cold, stop all dairy and the cold will dry up quickly. Miso soup is important because it contains the eight amino acids found in red meat. In a diet without red meat, miso is essential. Some people enjoy it in the morning, others during the day. Just try to have it every day, it's like a vitamin.

Speaking of vitamins, I for one believe balance is the important thing here. I don't believe you need fifteen vitamins a day. I do believe a few vitamins a day are an insurance policy. I take a vegetarian sugar-free multivitamin, Vitamin E (for skin and hair), and an iron tablet daily. Living in cities, traveling in planes, it's hard to be sure that we are not depleted. Vitamins give me that assurance. Again, be sure to purchase them at a health-food or vitamin store. Drug store vitamins are often sugar-coated and synthetic.

Before beginning the 30-Day Menu Plan, weigh yourself and measure your chest, waist, hips, thighs, calves, and arms. Record all of this information with the date. Weigh and measure yourself *only once a week* after that. Record your progress. If after the first week you do not see a change in weight, begin to write down everything you eat and drink all week long. Compare this with the 30-Day Menu Plan. If you stick to the natural way of eating, *you will lose weight.*

Flexibility

One of the reasons so many diets fail is that it is impossible to create one plan that totally suits each individual's tastes and needs. You should never feel forced to eat something you don't like or to be hungry because of lack of nourishment. I wish I could consult with each of my readers personally about their tastes, their needs. Since that is not possible you must use your own good judgment. You must be your own best friend.

Flexibility does not mean that a chocolate sundae can be substituted for a tossed salad. It does mean, however:

1. That all types of fresh vegetables are interchangeable;
2. That meals from different days can be interchanged as long as their calorie count is reasonably similar;
3. That timing of meals is adaptable to your schedule. If you hate breakfast, for instance, you can enjoy your first meal later in the day, perhaps during a break;

4. That if you dislike something you don't have to eat it. Use good judgment and replace it with something else.

Remember, *you* have to be the one with good judgment. There is no such thing as "cheating" on a diet because *you* are the only person who gains or loses. Your body won't lie. Stuff your mouth with midnite madness and it will show. Stick to good foods and you'll be showing off a new body in thirty days!

Beginning

The first step toward slimness is to read through this book. Familiarize yourself with the gentle mental guidelines, the natural kitchen and the 30-Day Plan. If you have read my previous books, *Getting into Your Wok with Annette Annechild* or *Wok Your Way Skinny*, you are already a Wokmaster, and some of the material will be familiar to you. It's a good idea to review that information as it will be so important to your success with the 30-Day Plan. For my accomplished Wokmasters the Plan begins in Chapter 5. It will take you through the month step by step with shopping lists, menus, and calorie counts. Some of the recipes will be familiar, many will be new. Be sure to try everything at least once and then substitute to suit your taste. For my new Wokmasters, each chapter will bring you a step further along into the world of natural eating. The first step will be purchasing and seasoning your wok, then mastering "The Basic Principle." In no time at all you'll be a Wokmaster and in thirty days, you'll even be a skinny one!

Working Out

If good food can be compared to high-test gasoline, exercise is equivalent to making sure the car gets started every day. Even if you're thin, without exercise the body will get loose and flabby. Exercise doesn't have to be an unpleasant activity. In fact just the opposite is true. Working out will get the juices flowing and make you feel energized. The important things are the type and amount of exercise you do. I've been an exercise teacher for the past fifteen years, and I think the biggest mistake people make is too much too quickly. If you are beginning an exercise program, the only positive way to embark on it is slowly. If you enter the activity very quickly and overly exert yourself, chances are you will tire of it all just as quickly and drop the whole idea. I feel the best way to prepare for any exercise program is to begin by stretching out the body. A yoga class is a wonderful way to learn how to stretch out the body as well as how to relax the mind. Stretching can be as simple as bending over from the waist and hanging there for three minutes. This stretches out the back of the legs, the shoulders, the back, and the neck. Try this upon awakening and before retiring, as well as before exercising strenuously.

A shoulder stand is a good stretch for the shoulders and neck. It also allows the blood to flow in the opposite direction to improve circulation and counteract the effects of gravity.

After the body is stretched, it is ready for a workout. Swimming, tennis, racketball, jogging, karate, calisthenics, walking, aerobics, and weights are all activities you might try. I work out with light weights every other day, and either jog or play tennis on the off days. I also dance as often as possible. The important thing is having a steady program. Very often investing in a private hour or two with a trainer to form your own personalized program is preferable to joining a health club or becoming part of a larger impersonal class. Never overexert yourself or push too hard. You can't shape up in an afternoon. A little patience, a steady program, and the body will respond beautifully.

In general, try to be as active and as aware of your body as possible. Take the stairs instead of the elevator, walk if you can to work or shop. Activity will greatly speed up the results of the 30-Day Menu Plan.

2
WHY A WOK?

A wok fits into this new way of eating because it is the easiest, fastest, most fun way I know of to make delicious meals that will produce a lean, taut body. *It* simplifies your kitchen as *you* simplify your life around eating. I just can't seem to be thin without one.

Woks lend themselves beautifully to the preparation of naturally slimming foods. Any vegetable can be stir fried in minutes and topped with a little cheese to serve as a delicious, satisfying meal. Fresh seafood can be steamed filleted or whole, poultry can be sliced and stir fried with vegetables to create interesting, delectable meals in minutes. All these dishes are low-calorie, high-energy meals. But when you start to taste how great they are, you won't be eating them because they're low in calories, you'll be eating them because you love how they *taste* and how you *feel* afterward.

And that's how you'll get thin, the easy way. When you start feasting on the good stuff, an occasional craving for junk will be fun to satisfy and guilt-free!

Whether you live alone or have a large family, it's easy to wok your way skinny. There's no better way for people, and especially children, to eat.

This style of cooking is as easy for many as it is for one. And the reward for everybody is a happy glow and a healthy, firm body.

Beginner or expert in the kitchen, with this book you can become a Wokmaster practically overnight.

Seasoning Your Wok

This is a most important first step, as seasoning your wok will prevent food from sticking to it. Here is an easy way to season a rolled-steel, nonelectric wok.

1. Before using, wash it thoroughly. This is the one time a scouring pad can be used on your wok. Woks are packed in machine oil, which is important to remove.
2. Place wok on its ring (the dok) over burner.
3. Then fill it with hot water and boil for at least two hours over high heat. As it is boiling, continue adding water to the brim; otherwise a watermark will form below the edge.
4. Pour out water. Repeat the process.
5. Dry wok completely over burner over high heat.
6. Next, with several thicknesses of paper toweling moistened with vegetable oil, rub the inside of the wok to close the pores. With fresh towels, repeat until the surface comes away clean. Do this process over medium heat. (Don't panic as you see black on the towels. It's not dirt—just the protective coating the wok is shipped in.)
7. When that's all off, you're ready to begin.
8. If by chance your wok has special or different instructions for seasoning, simply follow them.

Care of Your Wok

To clean wok after each use:

1. Wash with warm sudsy water, then scrub with bamboo brush (available at all housewares stores) or nylon pad.
2. Place wok on dok over burner in upright position.
3. *Dry immediately over high heat.*
4. Let cool down, and then rub lightly with 1 teaspoon of oil on a paper towel.

Be faithful in its care and you will be rewarded with a durable, well-seasoned wok.

Woks darken with use; that's part of their charm. They are cherished for their character and memories. You now own an heirloom!

Electric woks need no seasoning because they are precoated with an easy-to-clean, nonstick surface.

3
BECOMING A WOKMASTER

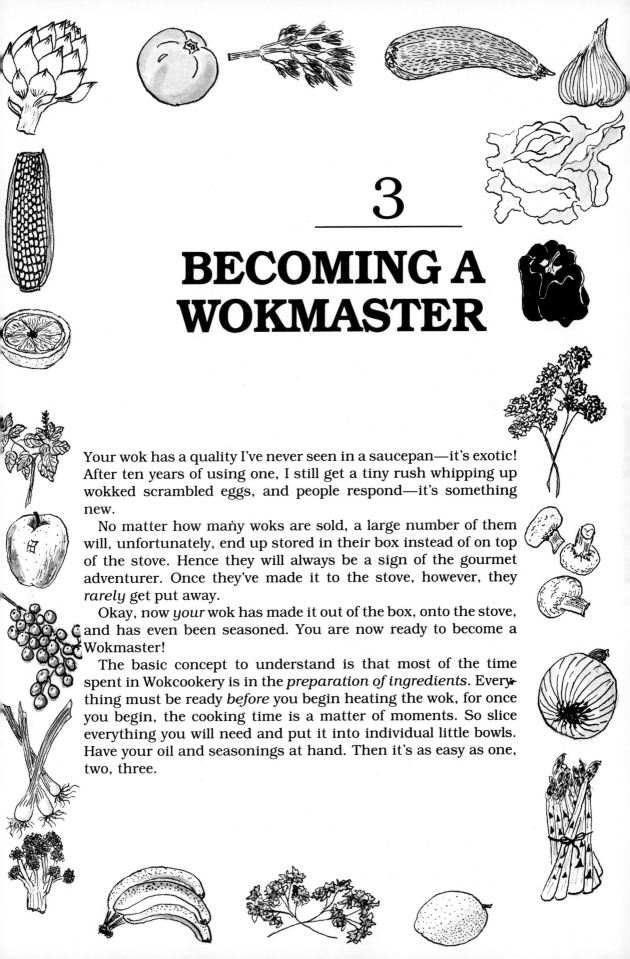

Your wok has a quality I've never seen in a saucepan—it's exotic! After ten years of using one, I still get a tiny rush whipping up wokked scrambled eggs, and people respond—it's something new.

No matter how many woks are sold, a large number of them will, unfortunately, end up stored in their box instead of on top of the stove. Hence they will always be a sign of the gourmet adventurer. Once they've made it to the stove, however, they *rarely* get put away.

Okay, now *your* wok has made it out of the box, onto the stove, and has even been seasoned. You are now ready to become a Wokmaster!

The basic concept to understand is that most of the time spent in Wokcookery is in the *preparation of ingredients*. Everything must be ready *before* you begin heating the wok, for once you begin, the cooking time is a matter of moments. So slice everything you will need and put it into individual little bowls. Have your oil and seasonings at hand. Then it's as easy as one, two, three.

The Basic Principle

One: Heat the wok over high heat.

Two: Once it is hot (two to three minutes), make a necklace of oil around the top of the wok. It will slide down, coating the sides and leaving a little pool in the bottom.

Three: Immediately start adding ingredients and stir.

Congratulations—you've begun!

A Word About HEAT

Wokcookery can be done over gas or electric heat. However, if you are using an electric stove, you must be especially careful about temperature control. Instead of preheating your wok over high heat, use medium-high, since it will be impossible to quickly bring the heat down. The dok is designed for both gas and electric stoves. For gas stoves, place the larger-diameter circle down; simply flip over for electric stoves.

Diagonal Slicing

Diagonal slicing is an Oriental tradition, and with good reason. By slicing with your knife at a 45-degree angle to the food, you produce thin slices that expose the largest possible area to heat, contributing to a fast cooking time. It is ideal in Wokcookery, since the cooking is done over high heat. Use this method for meats and fibrous vegetables, and it will also help tenderize them.

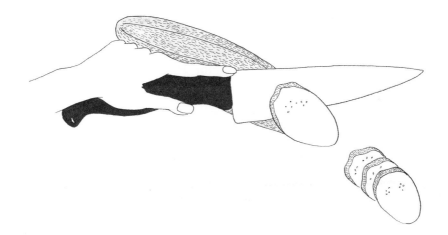

How to Like Cooking Better

A number-one rule—clean as you go.

I know it sounds like something you've heard all your life, but it's true. Not having to face a destroyed kitchen after each meal can improve your attitude about cooking in general. Cleaning as you go makes the cleanup occur when you're in a high-energy, *before*-dinner mood.

Basic Methods of Wokcookery

1. *Stir frying* is exactly that. It's simply heating the wok, necklacing with oil, and tossing in the vegetables. Stir to coat with oil and keep stirring until vegetables are firm but tender. This method prevents loss of vitamins in water and never lets veggies get limp. The color of the vegetables will actually deepen and brighten beautifully.

2. *Steaming.* For three dollars you can turn your wok into a hassle-free steamer. A stainless-steel insert can be purchased and fit right into your wok when you want to steam. You just boil water in the wok, put in the insert, lay your vegetables, fish, or whatever on top, and cover. I discovered a round cake rack also works fine, and you probably have one already. You can also buy tiered wooden steamers that work well and can steam several dishes at once. Your wok may have come with two wooden crisscrossed sticks for steaming. They fit in the bottom, and again, you boil water beneath them in the wok and lay vegetables across in a heatproof server. They work okay, but the three-dollar stainless-steel type can't be beat. Steaming adds no calories and also loses no vitamins.

3. *Deep Frying.* A wok makes deep frying a pleasure rather than an ordeal. For many reasons, it is absolutely the perfect tool for the job.

   It prevents spattering because of its shape and takes only 4 cups of oil (which is reusable) for a 14-inch to 16-inch wok. The intense and well-distributed heat immediately seals the nutrients and flavors into the food, assuring a light and especially delicate, nongreasy result. It also makes deep-fried food contain fewer calories, because there is no chance for the oil to be heavily absorbed.

   Secrets of successful deep frying are to have the batter and food ice cold and the oil very hot (375°F., 191°C on a deep-fat thermometer). Peanut oil is the best for deep frying since it will not smoke at this high temperature and also increases the nutritional value of the food.

4. *Poaching.* Poaching fish is an easy, fine-tasting method of preparation. It is especially good for the whole fish, but large thick fillets wrapped in a porous cloth will work well also. The wok's shape makes it ideal for poaching since the thickest part of the fish will be closest to the flame, allowing the whole fish to be cooked perfectly in the same amount of time.

   To Poach Fish: Bring enough water to totally cover fish by 1 inch to boil in your wok. Then lower the heat so that the water is just below the boiling point, and place the fish in the wok. Cover and adjust the heat to lowest possible setting. Cook ten minutes for a 12-inch fish, and lift out.

5. *Soup Making.* Because of its size and well-distributed heat, your wok is great for soups. However, if you are going to do a lot of soup making in the wok, I recommend your purchasing a second wok, for the long simmering process can eventually break down the patina (or seasoned surface). With two woks you can keep one for soup making, poaching, steaming, and reserve the other for stir frying and egg making.

6. *Barbecuing.* Take your wok outside and on the road! It works great over a barbecue grill or hibachi. When camping simply dig a fire pit and straddle the dok across it. Place the wok on the dok and you're all set.

How to Read a Recipe

In these carefully tested, original recipes you will find all the ingredients listed first, followed by the preparation, which is written simply step by step. So just . . .

1. Read through the recipe to get a general idea of the preparation.
2. Check to make sure you have all the ingredients.
3. Put all the ingredients out and have them ready as listed.
4. Follow the numerically listed steps.
5. Enjoy the tasty rewards.

A beginner in the kitchen or an expert can meet with fun and success. If you've got any ideas about being a lousy cook, just forget them! Anyone can do it, and you're already on your way!

4

THE NATURAL KITCHEN

The Natural Kitchen

A simple, clean kitchen is the best environment in which to embark on a program of cooking wholesome fresh foods. Some of the ingredients used in the 30-Day Menu Plan might be new to you, but I guarantee all of them are very worth trying. Searching out a well-stocked natural-food store in your area is a must. There's one there, I guarantee it. Check your local Yellow Pages to find where it's located.

The Kitchen Basics

One wok (or two): It's great to have two woks, but if one is what you are working with, make one dish first, place in a heatproof bowl, and place in warm oven if two woks are called for in the menu plan. Also, make sure you have a dok and cover for the wok.

A steamer rack: A small round cake-cooling rack or any commercial steamer works well.

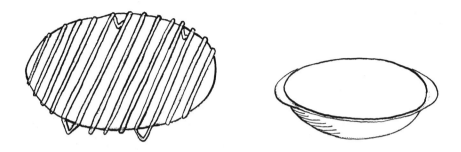

A sharp knife: A must for every chef. I like the self-sharpening type that is returned after use to its own holder.

A small utility knife is also useful.

A large, heavy pot: For pasta and rice making.

A small saucepan: For reheats and sauces.

A large cutting board: For all those fresh veggies.

A lettuce spinner: Available in heavy-duty plastic. Great for fresh, crisp salads.

Bowls: All kinds are great to have on hand. You will definitely need a large salad bowl, a large bowl for storing rice, and smaller bowls for sauces and soups.

Storage containers: Ziploc bags and plastic containers will keep foods fresh and appetizing.

Jars: For storing uncooked grains, flour, and seeds.

Roasting pans: For chickens and turkey.

Heatproof dish: For steaming or broiling fish. Choose one that fits on steamer rack in your wok.

Oil container: A mustard or ketchup squeeze bottle is perfect for necklacing your wok with oil.

Survival Recipes

Every week you should set a few hours aside to stock your kitchen with the basics for the week. Sunday is an ideal time to prepare weekly for the 30-Day Menu Plan.

Brown Rice

Try to always have brown rice in your refrigerator. It's great to include in any meal of the day. You can even turn it into a dessert! Keep it in the refrigerator loosely covered and it will last all week. If you are feeding a family, you may need to double the recipe or prepare it twice weekly. Forget white rice; it only makes you fat; brown rice cleanses the system.

1. Put 4 cups of water on to boil.
2. Rinse 2⅓ cups brown rice with cool water. Drain.
3. Put 1 tablespoon oil in a 2-quart pot. Heat over low flame.
4. Add rice and sauté until moisture is absorbed and rice smells nutty.
5. Add the 4 cups boiling water with 1 tablespoon tamari.
6. Do not stir. Allow to boil 3 minutes.
7. Cover and cook over *low* heat for 45 minutes. *Do not open or stir.*
8. After 45 minutes turn heat off, but allow to sit *unopened* for 15 minutes.
9. Fluff with fork.
10. Serve. It will stay warm a long time. To reheat, steam or stir fry.

General Note on Cooking Grains

When preparing grains, the rule of thumb is 2 parts water to 1 part grain, bring to boil and simmer, covered, until liquid is absorbed. Hot cereals can easily be prepared this way. A nice variation is substituting apple juice for part of the water. Millet and oats are excellent when prepared this way for breakfast and can always be used as an alternate breakfast in the Menu Plan. The addition of cinnamon, tofu, and fresh fruit is especially delicious.

How to Make Soup Stock

The best soups are made from homemade soup stocks. It's easy to have a stock always on hand. The first step is to save all your edible odds and ends. That means the tough stems from spinach, the peelings from onions and garlic, the discarded portions of vegetables such as cabbage cores or broccoli stalks. *Save everything* and keep it in a plastic bag in your refrigerator. Then one day a week when you're home for a few hours, simply:

1. Place the collected edibles in a large pot with an equal amount of water, measuring cup for cup.
2. Cover and simmer 45 minutes to 2 hours.
3. Strain, cool, and refrigerate or freeze.

This is the base for great soups and sauces, and it's filled with nutrients. Stock can also be made with chicken bones. Simply cover them with water, add your favorite seasonings, and boil covered for 1–2 hours. Strain and refrigerate or freeze. If you ever end up adding too much of one thing—ginger peel, for instance—you haven't ruined your stock. Just add more water. If it is still too strong, cut up one small onion and carrot. Add to stock and simmer for another 20–30 minutes. The taste should then be mellowed. Remember, you can use stock in place of water when preparing brown rice.

Potage de Garbage

Ingredients:

2 tablespoons oil
½ cup onions, chopped
½ cup carrots, sliced
5 cups garbage bag stock
1 bay leaf
leftover brown rice, bulgur, pasta (if spaghetti, cut into 1-inch pieces), or potatoes
any leftover cooked vegetables
leftover cooked meats or fish, diced
salt to taste
freshly ground pepper to taste
fresh parsley, chopped, to taste

1. Go through the refrigerator for leftovers. Use one starchy item (rice, bulgur, pasta, potatoes). Any combination of leftover vegetables that suits your fancy will work well. (If you have buttered your vegetables, place the leftovers in a colander and rinse briefly under hottest tap water to remove the butter.) Chicken and shellfish leftovers go well together, as do fish and shellfish. If you have both chicken and fish leftovers, do each of them a favor by using only one of them in your potage. Red meats such as beef, pork, and lamb (if you eat them) may be combined with each other or with chicken, but not with fish or shellfish. If you don't have a starch in your leftover bag and desire a heartier soup, just add a potato or two in step 4.
2. Heat wok over high heat and necklace with oil.
3. Add onions and carrots, and stir fry until onions are translucent and carrots are softened.
4. Add vegetable stock and bay leaf, lower heat, cover, and simmer 20 to 25 minutes until carrots are very tender.
5. Add leftovers you have collected in step 1. Simmer over medium heat uncovered for several minutes until leftovers are heated through.
6. Add salt and pepper to taste. Ladle into bowls and garnish with chopped fresh parsley.

Serves 4

Miso Soup

Miso is one of the most incredible foods ever invented [
Miso has a unique flavor that makes a great base for sou
also provides a healthful balance of essential oils, mineral
ural sugars, proteins, and vitamins.

It is a dark brown paste that is usually sold in plastic
in a health-food store. It's very different and *very* worth

One tip on miso soup making: Never let it boil once y
the miso paste. It destroys some of the most nutritional
able ingredients.

Miso is important in your daily diet. Try to always hav
hand.

It is also available in "instant packets" to be sipped like bouil-
lon.

Ingredients:

2 carrots
1 onion, or 1–2 scallions
¼ head cabbage
    sesame oil for cooking
5 cups stock or water
¼ teaspoon salt
4 tablespoons miso paste

1. Wash carrots and onion and thinly slice.
2. Wash cabbage and cut into strips.
3. Heat wok.
4. Necklace with oil.
5. Add carrots, onions, and cabbage. Stir fry for 10 minutes.
6. Add ½ cup stock or water, and bring veggies to boil.
7. Lower flame, cover, and simmer 15 minutes.
8. Add remaining stock and salt, and simmer 15 minutes.
9. Remove 1 ladle of stock and add miso paste to it. Stir till dissolved.
10. Add to wok. Stir. Cover and turn flame off.
11. Let set for 5 minutes, then serve.

Note: For variety, add mushrooms or squash (in step 5).

Yield: A wokful
Serves 6–8

Vegetable Miso Soup

Ingredients:

5 cups vegetable stock or water
oil for cooking
2 cloves garlic, minced (or ½ teaspoon bottled minced)
2 teaspoons fresh chopped ginger (optional)
1 small head broccoli, cut into small pieces
1 cup mushrooms, sliced
2 carrots, sliced
2 stalks celery, chopped
1 large onion or 3 scallions, chopped
1 cup tofu, diced
3 tablespoons miso (there are many different kinds of miso—experiment with them all)

1. Place 5 cups stock or water to boil in a large pot.
2. Heat wok.
3. Necklace with oil.
4. Add garlic and ginger, stir fry 30 seconds.
5. Add broccoli, mushrooms, carrots, celery, onion, and tofu to wok; stir fry 3–5 minutes.
6. When stock is boiling, add stir-fried vegetables. Simmer, covered, 15 minutes.
7. Remove one ladle of soup and place in small bowl.
8. Add miso to the bowl and stir till dissolved.
9. Add to soup pot. Stir and serve.

Remember never to boil miso; boiling destroys some of the nutritional content.

Yield: a wokful—
about 8 cups

A Shout About Sprouts!

What's packed with vitamin C, practically calorie-free, and able to grow in your kitchen cupboard? Sprouts—an amazing thing to know about, a virtual dieter's delight. Sprouts are the off-shoots of seeds and beans, and almost any of them can be sprouted. Super-energy food, sprouts can be added to almost any wokked dish, served as lettuce on a sandwich, or made into a lovely salad—and you can have a constant supply on your kitchen shelf! I've included simple instructions for growing your own; it's fun and easy. Alfalfa and mung bean sprouts can also be purchased packaged in natural-food stores.

Sprout It Yourself

The Jar Method:

You will need:
> seeds (about ¼ cup)
> 1 quart glass jar
> water
> 1 piece of cheesecloth or nylon netting
> 1 rubber band or canning jar ring

1. Put seeds in quart jar, cover with warm water, and soak overnight.
2. In the morning, place a piece of cheesecloth or nylon netting over the top of the jar, secure it with a rubber band or canning jar ring, and drain off excess water.
3. Put the jar on its side and place in a warm, dark place (like your cupboard).
4. Two or three times a day, rinse the seeds with water and drain well. Put the jar back on its side in the cupboard.
5. Your crop will be ready in three or four days. Then place the jar on the windowsill and let the sprouts have light for one day so they can begin making chlorophyll.
6. Eat and enjoy! Refrigerate those sprouts you're not going to eat at once and don't forget to begin the next crop!

Sprouts are ready to eat when they reach these sizes:

Alfalfa	1 inch	Mung	1½ to 2½ inches
Chick-peas	½ to ¾ inch	Soybean	½ inch
Flaxseed	¾ inch	Adzuki	½ inch
Lentil	1 inch		

The Story of Tofu

Have you ever been at an Oriental vegetable stand and noticed little white cakes floating in water? Ever wonder what they were? Well, they're tofu! And now tofu is available in most supermarkets.

Tofu is a fermented bean curd made from soybeans, and as strange as it sounds, tofu is really something very special. The texture is that of soft cheese and the flavor is fairly bland, but tofu's great asset is that it quickly absorbs the flavor of whatever it is in. Best of all, it is very high in protein and very low in calories! It also costs literally pennies to serve. I call it "future food" and predict that ten years from now almost everyone will know and appreciate tofu. It is really something to get hooked on. It is available in both large and small curd. The large squares are Japanese; the smaller, Chinese. Both have the same flavor, but the texture is a little different. I suggest you try them both. When I make spaghetti sauce, I always blend in chunks of tofu with the sauce to fortify a pasta dish with protein. It's also delicious blended as a salad dressing or vegetable dip.

The wonders of tofu are woven throughout this book. On the next page you'll find Tofu "Mayonnaise," a mock mayonnaise that's low in calories and delicious.

Note: Tofu should be stored in a container covered with fresh, cool water. Change the water every day. Storage time is one week for optimum flavor. It can also be frozen. To remove excess moisture from tofu cakes, place each cake on the underside of a flat-bottomed plate. Top with another flat-bottomed plate. Hold over sink at an angle and press plates firmly together until moisture stops dripping out.

To achieve a chewier texture with tofu, squeeze out moisture as described above. Wrap tofu so that it is airtight, and freeze for forty-eight to seventy-two hours. When ready to use, thaw tofu in refrigerator for six to eight hours or in a bowl of lukewarm water for one hour.

Tofu "Mayonnaise"

This one is a must try. It's high protein, low calorie, eggless "mayonnaise" that tastes so good you may never make the regular kind again!

Ingredients:

1 pound tofu (drained 15 minutes and squeezed—the more moisture you press or squeeze from the tofu the thicker the dressing will be)
⅓ cup fresh lemon juice, or more to thin dressing
2 teaspoons Dijon mustard
¼ teaspoon hot chili oil
¼ cup olive oil (optional: if you're watching calories closely you can omit the oil and it still tastes great)

1. With steel blade in place in a food processor*, crumble tofu into work bowl. Cover and process until completely smooth.
2. Scrape down sides of work bowl. Add lemon juice, mustard, and chili oil. Process 10 seconds or until well combined.
3. Add olive oil if desired. (It will give the dressing a bit more of a satiny texture plus the distinctive flavor of the oil.) Process 10 seconds.
4. Spoon into pint container and store tightly covered in the refrigerator.

Yield: 2 cups

Variations

1. *The simplest variation.* Substitute rice wine vinegar or a vinegar of your choice for the lemon juice, or use lime instead of lemon to give the dressing a special tang that goes well with salads containing fruit.
2. *Herb.* Add ¼ cup fresh (or 2 teaspoons dried) dill, basil, parsley, tarragon, or chervil when adding the lemon juice. Be creative and combine several of your favorite herbs to come up with your own "house" dressing. This and the following variations are best made several hours or a day in advance to allow the flavor to develop.
3. *Spinach.* Add ½ cup blanched, drained, and squeezed spinach to the work bowl with the crumbled tofu. Add ¼ tea-

*Can also be made in a blender.

spoon freshly grated nutmeg with the lemon juice. Excellent on cold poached fish.

4. *Garlic*. Add 4 large, peeled cloves and a 1-inch piece of peeled ginger root to the work bowl with the crumbled tofu. A tasty dip for fresh vegetables.

5. *Blue cheese*. If you like dressing smooth and creamy, add 2 ounces blue cheese or Gorgonzola to work bowl with the crumbled tofu. If you prefer it on the chunky side, add the cheese after all basic ingredients are smooth, and process briefly just to crumble cheese and distribute throughout the dressing. Try this over poached pears for an outstanding dessert.

Uma's Whole-Wheat Bread

Because I know that at least *once* in a great while you are going to insist on some bread, I am including bread to die for. It is the most delicious and nutritional bread imaginable. Go easy. Bread is fat food. Let a little go a long way and savor every speck of it.

Ingredients:

⅓ cup safflower oil
3 cups hot water
3 teaspoons salt, dissolved
⅓ cup honey
⅓ cup raw millet
1 cup sunflower seeds
½ cup sesame seeds
1 cup currants or raisins
1 tablespoon dry yeast in ½ cup lukewarm water (set aside)
10–11 cups whole-wheat flour

1. Mix first four ingredients in big bowl.
2. Add next four and stir again.
3. Add yeast to above mixture.
4. Add whole-wheat flour until you can't stir anymore—about 10 to 11 cups.
5. Knead until you're tired.
6. Let rise, punch down.
7. Place in 3 large, oiled loaf pans, and let rise again.
8. Bake in preheated oven at 400°F. for 10 minutes, then lower heat to 350° and bake for 40 more minutes.

Note: Add small pan of water in oven to keep bread moist.

Yields 3 large loaves

Ingredients

The backbone of any diet is the ingredients used in food preparation. The aim of this diet is to introduce you to a great variety of naturally low-calorie fresh foods Once you have wholeheartedly embarked on this new way of eating, you will be amazed at how delicious, filling, and easy to prepare your meals will be. Remember, this is a diet for the rest of your life.

Bulgur wheat: A flaked grain used in Tabouli Salad.

Breads: Be sure to check labels for sugar- and preservative-free varieties of whole wheat. Sprouted wheat-free bread is especially nutritious. Check your local natural-food store shelves.

Brown rice: An absolute must in your diet and not interchangeable with white rice. Available in natural food stores in short, medium, and long grain. Short is sweeter; long, fluffier.

Cereals: Shredded wheat is recommended because it is high in fiber and sugar-free. Brown rice cereal and Nutri-Grain flakes are also recommended. Beware of cereals that say "natural" and are filled with sugar. Check labels carefully.

Dairy products: All dairy intake should be *limited.* That means cheese, milk, eggs, yogurt, ice cream, etc.

Eggs: Buy fresh, organic, fertilized eggs if possible. These eggs come from chickens raised the old-fashioned way. Find them at your natural-food store and taste the difference.

Fish: Fresh fish is wonderfully low in calories and highly nutritious. Experiment with all varieties local to your area. Steam, poach, or boil.

Fruits: As a dessert, fruit is certainly preferable to sweet baked goodies, but the intake of fruit should be limited. Two pieces of fresh fruit are maximum in one day. Bananas are a good source of potassium.

Garlic, ginger root, onions: In the East these three foods are respected as "The Divine Trinity" for cleansing. They are very tasty too. Use as much as you like as often as you can. Garlic is now available minced and bottled. Be sure to get the refrigerated variety with no preservatives.

Grains: You need to have one every day. Try barley, millet, buckwheat, oats, rice, wheat berries, bulgur, and amaranth.

Honey: Buy unprocessed honey. Use it sparingly in place of sugar.

Lemons: Tasty and good for you. Use often.

Lettuce: Stay away from iceberg. Be sure to try all the other varieties as they are more nutritious than the popular iceberg variety.

Mayonnaise: See page 42 for Tofu "Mayonnaise." Try it, you'll like it.

Miso: Soybean paste that contains the eight essential amino acids found in red meat. Important to eat often either in soup or sauces.

Mustard: Dijon is an especially flavorful variety, a great alternative to butter when preparing sauces. Also add to salad dressings to cut down on oil. Again, check the labels for sugar and preservatives.

Oils: Be sure to buy unprocessed, unfiltered varieties. Stay away from "vegetable" oils. Try safflower, peanut, olive, and sesame.

Pepper: Much better for you than salt. Try cayenne, black, and white.

Pita: Low in calories, whole-wheat pita is better than bread in your daily diet.

Rice cakes: A great aid for dieters. Most brands have only thirty-five calories a cake. Delicious plain or with healthy toppings. Found in your supermarket or natural-food store.

Salad dressing: See page 66 for Claudette's Famous French Vinaigrette. When using bottled dressing be sure to purchase it at the natural-food store and use small amounts. In restaurants always order dressing and sauces "on the side."

Salt: Use only small amounts in cooking. Never put it on top of your food.

Seeds: Seeds such as sesame, poppy, and caraway are great tasting and high in protein. Sesame should be purchased unhulled and toasted in the oven or in a frying pan with no oil added.

Soup stock: Easy to make, great for your body. Use it as a base for poaching, sauces, and soups (see page 36).

Sprouts: High in protein and Vitamin C. Try different varieties. See page 40 for home sprouting.

Tahini: This is sesame paste, which is great in sauces. It is available in natural-food stores.

Tamari: A naturally processed soy sauce available in natural-food stores.

Tofu: I think of it as "future food." High in protein, low in calories, and very inexpensive. Use as much as possible. See page 41 for further information.

Vegetables: Buy often and a lot. Be creative—steam, bake, and stir fry them!

Vinegar: Low in calories and tasty. Try different varieties. My favorite is tarragon.

Wheat germ: Check label for sugar. Try toasted and raw.

Yogurt: Be sure to check labels for sugar. It's a good idea to buy plain yogurt and mix with fresh fruit, pureed or whole.

5

THE 30-DAY MENU PLAN

General Guidelines

Breakfast:

The basic menu for breakfast is:

Cottage Cheese with Fresh Fruit and Wheat Germ
Yogurt with Fresh Fruit and Wheat Germ
Cereal with Fresh Fruit and Milk
Eggs with 1 Slice Whole-Wheat Toast
Hot-cooked Cereals

The amounts are:

½ cup cottage cheese or yogurt
⅛ cup wheat germ
1 small peach; ½ banana; ½ cup blueberries, strawberries, or raspberries; ½ canteloupe; or a combination of an equal amount
⅔ cup cereal or cooked whole grains. Shredded wheat is recommended because it has no sugar and is high in fiber
1 cup skim milk—if you hate skim milk, use whole milk and use less. Also, raw milk is good to try
2 medium eggs or 1 large egg
1 slice whole-wheat toast—be sure to read the label to get a sugar- and preservative-free brand

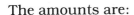

Lunch:

If you are lucky enough to be home for lunch, steamed fresh vegetables are always a good choice.

If you are out for lunch, a Garden Salad (but *not* a chef salad)—with the dressing on the side, used sparingly—is a good choice. A tuna, tofu, or turkey sandwich is a possible alternative, but beware heavy mayonnaise salads and try to eat only one slice of bread—be sure to specify whole-wheat. Sushi is another good alternative, also Thai or Chinese food; but forget the white rice. Steamed or broiled fish is also good; tell the waiter to hold the butter.

Dinner:

Try to eat dinner as early as possible (at least *before* 8 P.M.). If you are dining out, try to follow the diet-plan menu as closely as possible. (The suggestions above for lunch out are appropriate for dinner too.) Teach yourself that when dinner is over, food for the day has ended. Brush your teeth and wait for breakfast!

The general amount of fish and chicken is 6 ounces per person. Fresh steamed vegetables are unlimited. Rice is unlimited; calorie count is based on 1 cup.

SNACKS:

If you are very hungry between meals, allow yourself more food, but limit the choice to:

1. a piece of fresh fruit
2. a rice cake
3. a small bowl of brown rice
4. a steamed fresh vegetable
5. a tossed Garden Salad

LIQUIDS:

In the menu plan, no beverages are included. Your ideal choices for liquids are:

1. apple juice (unprocessed)
2. spring water
3. herb tea
4. Cafix (natural coffee)
5. vegetable juice

Occasionally you can allow yourself:

1. a glass of wine
2. a light beer

Note: Forget soda, diet soda, hard liquor, and coffee if possible. Try to drink twenty minutes before or after your meal; liquids dilute the stomach's digestive juices.

The Food Diary

A good idea for dieters. Try writing down everything you eat and compare this at the end of the day with the menu plan. Your food habits and patterns may surprise you.

THE PLAN

Next you will find the menus and recipes for the Thirty-Day Plan. Try to follow them as closely as possible for the best results. However, when you slip up and eat the wrong things, remember to be gentle with yourself. Realize that there are many needs we try to satisfy with food. Try to keep your thinking clear and start again the next day. All calorie counts are based on Barbara Kraus's book *Calories and Carbohydrates*.

Before each week's plan you will find a shopping list. No quantities are given because each person is feeding a different number of people with varying appetites. The list will remind you of all the things you will need for the week. Check the recipes beforehand and establish the quantities you will need. Ideally, this menu plan starts on Sunday, with Saturday as your shopping day. On Sunday you can prepare your rice and miso soup, and cut up your vegetables—this will make cooking during the week a breeze. *Bon appétit!*

SHOPPING LIST WEEK #1

FRESH PRODUCE

Acorn Squash

Artichokes
Beets
Broccoli
Cantaloupe
Carrots
Cucumbers
Fresh Dill
Fresh Fruit for Breakfast
Garlic
Grapefruit
Lemons (at least 6)

Lettuce (not iceberg, it's low nutritionally)
Mushrooms
Onions (Red and Yellow)
Parsley
Peppers
Potatoes (sweet or Idaho)
Scallions
Spinach
Sprouts
String Beans
Tomatoes
Zucchini

DAIRY

Cottage Cheese
Eggs
Milk

Mozzarella Cheese
Parmesan Cheese
Yogurt

STAPLES FROM NATURAL-FOOD STORE

Bran
Brown Rice (buy a few pounds)
Honey
Miso Paste and Instant Miso
Raisins
Rice Cakes
Sesame Seeds
Tahini

Tamari
Tofu
Tomato Sauce
Wheat Germ
Whole-Wheat Bread
Whole-Wheat Pasta
Whole-Wheat Pita Pockets

FRESH SEAFOOD AND POULTRY

Fish Fillets for Sunday
Chicken for Monday

Shrimp for Wednesday
Sole Fish Fillet for Thursday

STAPLES

Basil
Chili Powder
Curry Powder
Dijon Mustard
Dill
Mayonnaise
Olive Oil
Oregano
Peanut Oil

Pepper
Red Wine (optional)
Salt
Shredded Wheat Cereal
Tarragon (dried)
Tarragon Vinegar
Tuna (packed in water)
Walnuts

1

MENU

(Starts on Sunday)

BREAKFAST:

Cottage Cheese with Fresh Fruit and Wheat Germ
Calories: 150

LUNCH:

Steamed Sesame Spinach with Mushrooms and Tofu
Calories: 145

DINNER:

Artichoke with Mustard Sauce
Fresh Fish Fillet with Tahini Sauce
Fresh Beets with Lemon, Brown Rice
Calories: 425
Day's Total Calories: 774

DAY #1 RECIPES

BREAKFAST:

Cottage Cheese with Fresh Fruit and Wheat Germ

Ingredients:

      1 peach, or other fresh fruit
      ½ cup cottage cheese
      ⅛ cup wheat germ

1. Slice 1 rinsed peach, or other fresh fruit, into a small bowl.
2. Add 1 scoop (½ cup) cottage cheese.
3. Sprinkle with wheat germ (toasted tastes great, but avoid the sugared type).
4. Stir with spoon and enjoy.

Serves 1

LUNCH:

Steamed Sesame Spinach with Mushrooms and Tofu

Ingredients:

1 bunch fresh spinach
½ cup fresh mushrooms
4 ounces tofu
1 tablespoon tamari
1 teaspoon toasted sesame seeds
pepper to taste
juice of ½ lemon

1. Wash a bunch of fresh spinach *well*—it's sandy—but keep some water on leaves. Break off thick stems and discard (or save in a Ziploc bag for soup stock).
2. Slice mushrooms. Set aside.
3. Cube tofu cake. Set aside.
4. Heat wok over high heat.
5. Toss in spinach and mushrooms, lower heat to medium, and cover.
6. Meanwhile, toss tofu cubes with tamari and toasted sesame seeds in small bowl.
7. After 3 minutes, remove wok cover and add tofu. Stir and cover for 2 more minutes.
8. Sprinkle with pepper. Pour lemon juice over. Toss and serve.

Serves 1

Artichokes with Mustard Sauce

1. First rinse artichokes in cool water. Drain by turning upside down.
2. Clip tips of leaves with scissors to debarb, and cut thick stem at base so that the artichoke will stand upright.
3. Boil 2 inches water in deep pot and stand artichokes up in it. Cover and cook about 45 minutes for large artichokes, 35 for small.

I used frozen & poured sauce over. cut mustard sauce in ½.

Serves 2

Mustard Sauce

Ingredients:

2 tablespoons Dijon mustard
2 tablespoons fresh lemon juice
1 tablespoon fresh parsley, chopped
1 teaspoon olive oil
  salt and pepper to taste

1. Combine all ingredients.
2. Use as a dip for your artichoke leaves, and forget the idea of melted butter!

Serves 2

Fresh Fish Fillets with Tahini Sauce

Ingredients:

2 6-ounce fish fillets
  oil for greasing pan

1. Rinse fillets. Pat dry.
2. Place in greased heatproof dish.
3. Brush with Tahini Sauce (recipe below).
4. Steam, or broil, till fish flakes gently with fork, about 3 to 8 minutes.

Serves 2

Tahini Sauce

Ingredients:

½ teaspoon tahini
½ teaspoon Dijon mustard
½ teaspoon mayonnaise

1. Combine all ingredients and stir.
2. Brush on fish.

Fresh Beets with Lemon

Ingredients:

fresh beets, 1 bunch (about 5—small ones are more tender)
juice of 1 lemon
pepper to taste

1. Put a large pot of water on to boil.
2. Wash and remove stems and leaves of beets, leaving 2 inches of stem with beet. Save leaves for another meal. They are delicious steamed.
3. When water is boiling, add beets and cover.
4. Cook till tender when pierced with fork.
5. Peel and slice.
6. Pour lemon juice over, add pepper to taste, and serve.

Note: If you wish to prepare beets ahead of time, leave beets after step 4 until needed; then peel, slice, and sauté with juice of 1 lemon over low heat in wok. Sprinkle with pepper and serve.

Serves 2

Brown Rice

See page 35.

DAY #

2
MENU

BREAKFAST:

Cantaloupe Half with Cottage Cheese
Calories: 143

LUNCH:

Tuna Salad in Whole-Wheat Pita Pocket
Calories: 194

DINNER:

Roast Lemon Chicken
Baked Potatoes
Stir-Fried String Beans with Garlic
Calories: 595
Day's Total Calories: 932

DAY #2 RECIPES

BREAKFAST:

Cantaloupe Half with Cottage Cheese

Ingredients:

½ cantaloupe
½ cup cottage cheese

1. Scoop seeds from halved melon.
2. Place ½ cup-scoop cottage cheese in center. Enjoy!

Serves 1

LUNCH:

Tuna Salad in Whole-Wheat Pita Pocket

Ingredients:

1 can solid white tuna packed in water
1 tablespoon mayonnaise
1 teaspoon Dijon Mustard
  juice of ½ lemon
3 walnuts, chopped finely
  pinch dill
  pinch pepper
1 whole-wheat pita pocket

1. Mix together well. Use one-half for sandwich in pita bread.

Serves 1

Roasted Lemon Chicken

Ingredients:

    1 roasting chicken
1—2 lemons
    2 cloves garlic, skins removed

1. Rinse chicken with cool water. Drain and pat dry.
2. Place in greased roasting pan.
3. Slice lemons in half and pierce with fork.
4. Stuff lemons inside cavity with garlic.
5. Preheat oven to 450°F. Place chicken in the oven. Turn down heat immediately, and bake at 350°F. till done, basting occasionally. (Allow about 20 minutes a pound for a chicken weighing up to 6 pounds.)
6. Serve with the lemony gravy at the bottom of the pan.
7. Dieters skip the gravy and the *skin*.

Note: Buy a larger chicken than you will need, because leftover chicken is required for Day #3 Lunch.

Serves 2 with leftovers

Baked Potatoes

Ingredients:

   2 yams or sweet potatoes
     aluminum foil
   1 teaspoon butter

1. Scrub 2 potatoes well. Preferably use sweet potatoes. Otherwise, Idaho are a good choice.
2. Wrap them in foil, pierce with fork.
3. Place in oven with chicken at 350°F. for last hour of cooking.
4. Remember—only *1 teaspoon* of butter when you eat the potato! Be sure to eat skin as many vitamins are stored there.

Serves 2

Stir-Fried String Beans with Garlic

Ingredients:

   ½ pound string beans
   1 teaspoon olive oil
   1 teaspoon minced garlic (The bottled garlic in oil now available at your grocer's does make it easy. Be sure to buy the refrigerated variety with no preservatives.)

1. Rinse beans and snap off strings at ends.
2. Heat wok with steamer inserted and 1 cup water underneath.
3. When water boils, add beans. Cover and steam about 15 minutes, or until crisp-tender.
4. Empty water from wok. Dry wok over high heat. When dry add 1 teaspoon olive oil.
5. Add garlic and sauté 30 seconds.
6. Add beans, stir fry 2 to 3 minutes more.
7. Serve.

Serves 2

DAY #

3
MENU

BREAKFAST:

Shredded Wheat Cereal with Fresh Fruit and Skim
Milk
Calories: 207

LUNCH:

Stanley's Chunky Chicken Salad in Whole-Wheat Pita
Pocket
Calories: 288

DINNER:

Tofu-Stuffed Bell Peppers
Tossed Garden Salad
Stir-Fried Zucchini Parmesan
Calories: 475
Day's Total Calories: 970

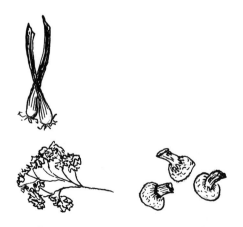

DAY #3 RECIPES

BREAKFAST:

Shredded Wheat Cereal with Fresh Fruit and Skim Milk

Ingredients:

⅔ cup shredded wheat (or other natural non-sugared cereal)
½ banana or peach (or ½ cup fresh berries)
1 cup skim milk (or ½ cup whole milk)
1 teaspoon honey (optional)

Note: If you must have a sweetener, use 1 teaspoon honey.

Serves 1

LUNCH:

Stanley's Chunky Chicken Salad in Whole-Wheat Pita Pocket

Ingredients:

½ cup chicken pieces from Day #2 Dinner
1 teaspoon mustard
1 teaspoon mayonnaise
pinch dried dill
pinch dried tarragon
salt and pepper to taste
lettuce leaves
1 whole-wheat pita pocket

1. Combine first six ingredients.
2. Stuff into pita pocket, add lettuce leaves, and enjoy.

Serves 1

Tofu-Stuffed Bell Peppers

Delicious and can be made in advance, refrigerated or frozen!

Ingredients:

>   4 peppers
>   4–6 fresh mushrooms
>   1 clove garlic, or ½ teaspoon minced bottled garlic
>   1 small onion
>   4 ounces tofu
>   2 cups tomato sauce
>   pinch dried oregano
>   pinch dried basil
>   pinch salt and pepper to taste
>   1 tablespoon red wine (optional)
>   2 teaspoons olive oil
>   1 teaspoon toasted sesame seeds
>   1 teaspoon wheat germ
>   1 cup cooked rice

1. Wash peppers and cut off tops. Remove seeds and membranes and discard.
2. Steam peppers in ½ inch water for 4 to 6 minutes.
3. Slice mushrooms, mince garlic, dice onion, cut tofu into chunks.
4. In saucepan, heat tomato sauce with oregano, basil, salt and pepper, and red wine, if using.

5. Heat wok.
6. Necklace with 2 teaspoons olive oil.
7. Add garlic, onions, and mushrooms. Stir fry 1 minute and add tofu, sesame seeds, and wheat germ. Sprinkle with salt and pepper. Stir fry till onions are almost tender and tofu slightly browned.
8. Add ½ the sauce and all the rice to wok. Mix well.
9. Place a little sauce in bottom of baking pan. Stand peppers upright and fill with rice mixture.
10. Pour rest of sauce over peppers.
11. Bake at 350°F. for 30 minutes. Serve.

Serves 4

Stir-Fried Zucchini Parmesan

Ingredients:

oil for cooking
1 clove garlic, minced, or ½ teaspoon minced bottled garlic
2 small zucchini, thinly sliced
salt and pepper to taste
⅛ teaspoon dried oregano
⅛ cup grated Parmesan cheese

1. Heat wok.
2. Necklace wok with oil.
3. Add garlic and zucchini, and stir fry. Sprinkle with salt, pepper, and oregano.
4. When crisp and golden, remove and top with grated Parmesan cheese.
5. Serve.

Serves 2 with leftovers

Tossed Garden Salad

Ingredients:

      lettuce (romaine, Boston, or Bibb)
1 tomato
2 carrots, shredded or sliced
1 small red onion (optional)
½ cucumber, sliced

My friend Claudette Kriegel-Baruc taught me how to make the best dressing in the world. She says the trick is making it in the bottom of the salad bowl instead of pouring it over the salad. Be sure to try it, that way you'll need much less dressing for your salad.

Claudette's Famous French Vinaigrette

Ingredients:

2 tablespoons olive oil
1–2 teaspoons tarragon vinegar
1 sprinkle garlic, powdered or minced
   salt and pepper to taste

1. Mix all ingredients with fork *in bottom of salad bowl.*
2. Add salad ingredients and toss well.
(Try adding 1 teaspoon Dijon mustard for variety.)

Serves 2

4
MENU

BREAKFAST:

Fresh Grapefruit Half
Zucchini and Eggs
1 Slice Whole-Wheat Toast
Calories: 294

LUNCH:

Tossed Garden Salad with Rice Cake
Calories: 200

DINNER:

Shrimp and Vegetable Fried Rice
Calories: 350
Day's Total Calories: 844

DAY #4 RECIPES

BREAKFAST:

Fresh Grapefruit Half

Ingredients:

½ fresh grapefruit

1. Section and serve (don't add sugar!).

Zucchini and Eggs

Ingredients:

2 small or 1 large egg(s)
1 tablespoon milk
  salt and pepper to taste
1 small zucchini
1 scallion (optional)
1 tablespoon oil
1 teaspoon toasted sesame seeds
1 slice toasted whole-wheat bread

1. In small bowl, combine egg and milk; beat with whisk or fork. Season with salt and pepper and set aside.
2. Slice zucchini into thin slices. Chop scallion, if using.
3. Heat wok over high heat.
4. Necklace with 1 tablespoon oil.
5. Add zucchini and stir fry.
6. Season with sesame seeds and scallion, if using.
7. When zucchini is lightly browned and tender, add eggs. Keep stirring.
8. When eggs reach desired consistency, lift out and enjoy with 1 slice whole-wheat toast.

Serves 1

LUNCH:

Tossed Garden Salad with Rice Cake

See Day #3 Dinner. If taking to work, pack salad and dressing separately. Toss when ready to eat. Enjoy with a rice cake.

Serves 1

DINNER:

Shrimp and Vegetable Fried Rice

Ingredients:

         1 small onion
            oil for cooking
      ¾ cup fresh or frozen shrimp, shells removed
         1 cup broccoli, cut into thin spears
      1½ cups cooked brown rice
         1 small handful sprouts
      1–2 tablespoons tamari

1. Cut onion into thin slices.
2. Heat wok.
3. Necklace with oil.
4. Add shrimp, stir fry only till pink, and remove.
5. Add broccoli and onion to wok, stir fry 4 to 5 minutes.
6. Add rice and sprouts, and season with tamari.
7. Add shrimp, stir to heat thoroughly, and serve.

Serves 1

DAY #

5
MENU

BREAKFAST:

Shredded Wheat Cereal with Fresh Fruit and Skim
Milk
Calories: 207

LUNCH:

Tofu Salad Delight with Lettuce and Tomato on
Whole-Wheat Pita
Calories: 229

DINNER:

Fresh Asparagus with Lemon
Steamed Sole with Dill Sauce
Tossed Garden Salad
Calories: 340
Day's Total Calories: 776

DAY #5 RECIPES

BREAKFAST:

Shredded Wheat Cereal with Fresh Fruit and Skim Milk

See Day #3 Breakfast.

LUNCH:

Tofu Salad Delight

Ingredients:

    4 ounces tofu
    1 tablespoon mayonnaise
    1 teaspoon Dijon mustard
    1 tablespoon tamari
    3 walnuts, chopped
      pinch of dried dill
      pinch of black pepper
      lettuce
      tomato
    1 whole-wheat pita pocket

1. Combine tofu, mayonnaise, mustard, tamari, walnuts, dill, and pepper, and stuff into pita pocket with lettuce, tomato, and sprouts.
2. Enjoy!

Serves 1

Fresh Asparagus
with Lemon

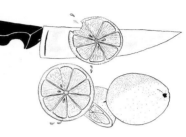

Ingredients:

½ pound asparagus
juice of 1 lemon

1. Rinse asparagus and cut off stalky ends.
2. Steam in wok, with fish if you like (see recipe below), till crisp-tender, about 3 to 5 minutes.
3. Pour lemon juice over.
4. Have all you want!

Serves 1

Steamed Sole with Dill Sauce

Ingredients:

small bunch fresh dill
½ bunch fresh parsley
juice of ½ lemon
1 tablespoon mayonnaise
½ pound sole or flounder

1. Remove dill from stem and process in blender or food processor with parsley, lemon, and mayonnnaise.
2. Place fish in greased heatproof plate and brush on sauce.
3. Fish can be steamed with asparagus over water in wok until fish flakes easily with fork (about 10–15 minutes).

Tossed Garden Salad

See Day #3 Dinner.

Serves 1

BREAKFAST:

Yogurt with Fresh Fruit and Wheat Germ
Calories: 204

LUNCH:

Christopher's Tuna Delight in Whole-Wheat Pita
Pocket
Calories: 194

DINNER:

Pasta Primavera
Calories: 400
Day's Total Calories: 798

DAY #6 RECIPES

BREAKFAST:

Yogurt with Fresh Fruit and Wheat Germ

1. Mix ½ cup plain yogurt with fresh fruit.
2. Stir in wheat germ.
3. Serve.

Serves 1

LUNCH:

Christopher's Tuna Delight in Whole-Wheat Pita Pocket

Ingredients:

    1 7-ounce can solid white tuna packed in water
    1 tablespoon mayonnaise
    1 teaspoon Dijon mustard
      juice of ½ lemon
    3 walnuts, finely chopped
      pinch dried dill
      pinch black pepper
    1 whole-wheat pita pocket

1. Mix first seven ingredients together well, and use half for 1 sandwich in pita pocket.
2. Serve.

Serves 1

DINNER:

Pasta Primavera

Ingredients*:

      salt
      oil for cooking
  2 cloves garlic, minced (or ½–¾ teaspoon minced bottled garlic)
  1 zucchini, thinly sliced
  2 scallions, chopped
      pepper to taste
  1 cake tofu (4 ounces), cubed
  6 ounces whole-wheat pasta
  1 cup tomato sauce

1. Put large pot of water on to boil for pasta. Add salt to water.
2. Heat wok over high heat.
3. Necklace with oil.
4. Add garlic, zucchini, and scallions to wok. Stir fry.
5. Sprinkle with salt and pepper.
6. Add tofu and stir. Lower heat and cover.
7. Cook pasta according to directions.
8. When pasta is *al dente,* drain well. Mix with tomato sauce and top with veggies.

Note: Buy and defrost turkey in refrigerator for use on Sunday.

Serves 1

* Any vegetable you'd like to add is fine; simply mince and stir fry.

BREAKFAST:

Cottage Cheese with Fresh Fruit and Wheat Germ
Calories: 150

LUNCH:

Tofu Burgers in Whole-Wheat Pita Pocket
Calories: 379

DINNER:

Lisa's Rice-Stuffed Acorn Squash
Calories: 300
Day's Total Calories: 829

DAY #7 RECIPES

Cottage Cheese with Fresh Fruit and Wheat Germ

See Day #1 Breakfast.

Tofu Burgers in Whole-Wheat Pita Pocket

Ingredients:

1 large cake tofu, 6 ounces (or 2 Chinese small curd cakes), drained and crumbled
½ cup bran
¼ cup wheat germ
2 tablespoons tamari or soy sauce
¼ teaspoon chili powder, or to taste
½ cup carrots, shredded
1 scallion, finely miced
  oil for cooking
4 small whole-wheat pita pockets or 2 large pockets cut in half
1 cup sprouts
4 tomato slices

1. Press excess water from tofu.
2. Place tofu in bowl and crumble with fork.
3. Add bran, wheat germ, tamari, chili powder, carrots, and scallion. Mix well and form into 4 patties.
4. Heat wok.
5. Necklace with oil.
6. When oil is hot, place patties in 2 at a time.
7. Flip when golden (about 2 to 3 minutes).
8. Remove patties and place on platter in warm oven. Repeat till all patties are done
9. Serve inside pita pockets topped with sprouts, tomato slices, and perhaps a tablespoon of your favorite salad dressing or condiment.

Serves 2

DINNER:

Lisa's Rice-Stuffed Acorn Squash

Ingredients:

1 large acorn squash
oil for cooking
½ cup sliced mushrooms
¼ cup coarsely chopped walnuts, plus a few whole for garnish
¼ cup raisins
1–1½ cups cooked brown rice

1. Cut acorn squash in half lengthwise and clean out seeds and membrane. Steam face down 20–25 minutes or till tender when pierced with fork. Put aside.
2. Meanwhile, heat wok.
3. Necklace with oil.
4. Stir fry mushrooms 1 minute and add nuts and raisins.
5. Stir fry together 1 minute and add rice. Stir to combine.
6. Season with tamari.
7. When squash is ready, stuff with rice mixture. Garnish with whole walnuts and serve.

Any extra filling can be served on the side.

Serves 2

SHOPPING LIST WEEK #2

Note: Be sure to check what you have on hand before shopping, and remember quantities will vary according to number of people you are feeding.

FRESH PRODUCE

Artichoke
Avocado
Broccoli
Carrots
Cucumbers
Dill
Fresh Fruit for Breakfast
Garlic
Ginger Root
Grapefruit
Horseradish (optional)
Lemons
Lettuce
Limes
Mushrooms
Onions
Potatoes (sweet or Idaho)
Scallions
Snow Peas
Spinach
Sprouts (Mung and Alfalfa)
Tomatoes
Turnips
Your Choice of Additional Vegetables for Stir-Frying as a Side Dish
Zucchini

DAIRY

Cottage Cheese
Eggs
Milk
Yogurt

FRESH SEAFOOD AND POULTRY

Turkey for Sunday (Chicken may be substituted)
Shrimp for Tuesday
Swordfish for Wednesday
Salmon for Thursday
Boneless Breast of Chicken for Friday
Mussels and Boneless Chicken Breast for Saturday

STAPLES FROM NATURAL FOOD STORE

Brown Rice (keep a few pounds on hand)
Bulgur (keep a few pounds on hand)
Miso Paste
Rice Cakes
Sesame Seeds
Tahini
Tamari
Tofu
Wheat Germ
Whole-Wheat Bread
Whole-Wheat Pita Pockets

STAPLES

Capers
Cashews
Cayenne Pepper
Chicken Stock (homemade or canned)
Chives
Dijon Mustard
Dill
Hot Chili Oil or Tabasco
Mayonnaise
Olive Oil
Oyster Sauce
Peanut Oil
Shredded Wheat Cereal
Tarragon (dried)
Tarragon Vinegar
Tuna (packed in water)

DAY #

8
MENU

BRUNCH:

Fresh Grapefruit Half
Scallioned Sesame Eggs, 1 Slice Whole-Wheat Toast
Calories: 294

DINNER:

Roast Turkey, Baked Potatoes
Stir-Fried Fresh Vegetables
Calories: 500
Day's Total Calories: 794

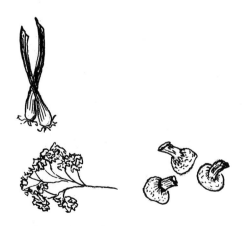

DAY #8 RECIPES

BRUNCH:

Fresh Grapefruit Half

See Day #4 Breakfast.

Scallioned Sesame Eggs

Ingredients:

    1 scallion
    4 eggs
    1 tablespoon milk or water
      salt and pepper to taste
      oil for cooking
    1 teaspoon sesame seeds
    1 slice whole wheat bread

1. Rinse and chop scallion. Set aside.
2. Beat eggs with milk or water, salt, and pepper.
3. Heat wok.
4. Necklace with oil.
5. Add scallion and sesame seeds and stir fry for 2 to 3 minutes.
6. Add eggs and continue stirring until they are desired consistency.
7. Lift out and enjoy. Serve with 1 slice whole-wheat toast.

Serves 2

Roast Turkey

Ingredients:

       turkey giblets
   4 cloves garlic
   4 cups water
       whole turkey

1. Remove giblets and place with garlic in large saucepan. Cover with 4 cups water and bring to boil. Then simmer. This will be used for basting.
2. Put bird on rack uncovered in oven preheated to 450°F.
3. Reduce heat immediately to 350°F. Baste frequently.
4. Cook 20 minutes per pound for an unstuffed bird. For a bird weighing 18 to 25 pounds, reduce heat to 300°F. and cook 13 to 18 minutes per pound.
5. Allow to cool half hour before slicing. Don't eat the skin!

Baked Potatoes

See Day #2 Dinner.

Stir-Fried Fresh Vegetables

Ingredients:

   oil for cooking
   your choice of fresh seasonal vegetables, cut into small pieces (zucchini, onion, and red pepper are a nice combination—be creative!)
   tamari to taste

1. Heat wok.
2. Necklace with oil.
3. Add vegetables and stir until crisp-tender.
4. Season with tamari to taste and serve.

Note: Don't forget to make rice for this week.

Can be made for 1 to 6 persons

BREAKFAST:

Shredded Wheat Cereal with Banana and Skim Milk
Calories: 207

LUNCH:

Tossed Garden Salad with Tofu Chunks and Rice
Cake
Calories: 200

DINNER:

Stir-Fried Turkey and Broccoli in Oyster Sauce with
Brown Rice
Calories: 320
Day's Total Calories: 727

DAY #9 RECIPES

BREAKFAST:

Shredded Wheat Cereal with Banana and Skim Milk

See Day #3 Breakfast.

LUNCH:

Tossed Garden Salad with Tofu Chunks

Add 4 ounces tofu cut into chunks to Tossed Garden Salad. See Day #3 Dinner.

Serves 1

Stir-Fried Turkey and Broccoli in Oyster Sauce with Brown Rice

Ingredients:

    2 cups cooked brown rice
      oil for cooking
1–2 cups broccoli, cut in small pieces
    1 scallion, chopped
    1 cup leftover turkey pieces
1–2 tablespoons oyster sauce

1. Before starting, place ¼ cup water and 2 cups cooked brown rice in saucepan. Heat over low heat.
2. Heat wok.
3. Necklace with oil
4. Add broccoli and scallion. Stir fry 3 minutes.
5. Add turkey. Stir.
6. Add oyster sauce to taste.
7. Serve over brown rice.

Note: If you have any free time, place turkey carcass in large pot covered with water. Add seasonings (1 bay leaf; ½ teaspoon oregano, basil and thyme; 2 cloves garlic). Simmer 1 to 2 hours for stock. Strain and freeze.

Serves 2

DAY
10
MENU

BREAKFAST:

Yogurt with Fresh Fruit and Wheat Germ
Calories: 204

LUNCH:

Turkey Salad in Pita Pocket
Calories: 229

DINNER:

Ginger Cashew Shrimp with Brown Rice
Calories: 310
Day's Total Calories: 743

DAY #10 RECIPES

BREAKFAST:

Yogurt with Fresh Fruit and Wheat Germ

See Day #6 Breakfast.

LUNCH:

Turkey Salad in Pita Pocket

Ingredients:

>   ¾ cup leftover turkey
>   1 teaspoon Dijon mustard
>   1 tablespoon mayonnaise
>   pinch dried tarragon
>   salt and pepper to taste
>   1 whole-wheat pita pocket
>   lettuce and tomato (optional)

1. Mix first five ingredients and stuff into pita.
2. Top with lettuce and tomato if desired.

Serves 1

 *very good*

Cashew Ginger Shrimp with Brown Rice

Ingredients:

          1 cup cooked brown rice
             oil for cooking
          1 clove garlic, minced, or ½ teaspoon minced bottled garlic
      1–2 slices fresh ginger root, minced
          1 scallion, chopped
          ½ pound fresh shrimp, shelled
          1 cup snow peas
          ⅛ cup cashews
          ½ teaspoon cayenne pepper (optional) *– to taste*
          1 teaspoon fresh lime or lemon juice
             tamari to taste

1. Before starting, heat 1 cup cooked brown rice in saucepan over low heat with ¼ cup water.
2. Heat wok.
3. Necklace with oil.
4. Add garlic, ginger, and scallion. Stir fry 30 seconds.
5. Add shrimp. Stir fry 30 seconds.
6. Add all other ingredients.
7. When shrimp are pink, the dish is ready. Serve over brown rice.

Serves 1

BREAKFAST:

Sprout and Carrot Omelet
with Brown Rice
Calories: 240

LUNCH:

Avocado with Lettuce, Tomato, and Sprouts in Whole-
Wheat Pita Pocket
Calories: 279

DINNER:

Swordfish Steak with Capers
Fresh Turnips with Chives
Hot Lemon Spinach and Mushrooms
Calories: 435
Day's Total Calories: 954

DAY #11 RECIPES

Sprout and Carrot Omelet

Ingredients:

> oil for cooking
> 2 carrots, grated
> 1 small onion, minced
> 1 tablespoon toasted sesame seeds
> 1 handful alfalfa or mung bean sprouts
> 4 eggs, beaten
> salt and pepper to taste
> heated brown rice

1. Heat wok.
2. Necklace lightly with oil.
3. Stir fry carrots and onion till tender.
4. Add sesame seeds and sprouts and stir fry.
5. Add eggs. Season with salt and pepper.
6. Keep eggs moving around in wok.
7. Cook till desired consistency and serve with brown rice.

Serves 2

LUNCH:

Avocado with Lettuce, Tomato, and Sprouts in Whole-Wheat Pita Pocket

Ingredients:

> ½ avocado
> 1 whole-wheat pita pocket
> 1 leaf lettuce
> 1–2 slices tomato
> handful sprouts
> freshly ground pepper to taste
> squeeze of fresh lemon

1. Slice half of an avocado and place in whole-wheat pita pocket.
2. Add lettuce, tomato, and sprouts.
3. Add freshly ground pepper and a squeeze of lemon, and enjoy.

Serves 1

DINNER:

Swordfish Steak with Capers

Ingredients:

1 teaspoon mayonnaise
2 6-ounce swordfish steaks
1 small lemon
1 tablespoon capers
freshly grated horseradish (optional)

1. Lightly brush the mayonnaise on both sides of the swordfish.
2. Place on broiling rack or barbecue grill.
3. Broil or grill for 5 minutes and flip over.
4. Pour lemon juice over and top with capers.
5. Broil or grill 5 to 8 more minutes and serve, with freshly grated horseradish if you like.

Serves 2

Fresh Turnips with Chives

Ingredients:

2 large turnips
oil for cooking
1 tablespoon dried chives, chopped
juice of ½ lemon
freshly ground pepper

1. Wash turnips and steam for 3 to 5 minutes or until tender when pierced with a fork.
2. Slice and set aside till almost ready to dine.
3. Then heat wok.

4. Necklace with oil.
5. Sauté turnips to heat through.
6. Sprinkle with chives and pepper.
7. Pour lemon juice over and serve.

Serves 2

Hot Lemon Spinach and Mushrooms

Ingredients:

> 1 pound fresh spinach
> ½ pound fresh mushrooms
> 1 clove garlic, or ½ teaspoon minced bottled garlic
>   oil for cooking
> 1 tablespoon sesame seeds
>   salt and pepper to taste
>   juice of 1 lemon

1. Wash spinach well, it's sandy. Clip stalky stems and set aside.
2. Brush mushrooms well. Trim stalk and slice vertically. Set aside.
3. Mince garlic. Set aside.
4. Heat wok.
5. Necklace with oil.
6. Add sesame seeds and garlic and stir fry till golden.
7. Add mushrooms, toss, and stir fry 3 minutes.
8. Add spinach, toss and cover.
9. As spinach cooks down, sprinkle with salt and pepper, and pour lemon juice over.
10. Serve.

Note: If you have only 1 wok, the turnips can be done in a frying pan.

Serves 2

BREAKFAST:

Cottage Cheese with Fresh Fruit and Wheat Germ
Calories: 150

LUNCH:

Brown Rice Vegetable Salad (or Dinner Leftovers)
Calories: 225

DINNER:

Poached Salmon with Yogurt-Dill Sauce
Garden Salad
Baked Potatoes
Calories: 500
Day's Total Calories: 875

DAY #12 RECIPES

BREAKFAST:

Cottage Cheese with Fresh Fruit and Wheat Germ

See Day #1 Breakfast.

LUNCH:

Brown Rice Vegetable Salad

Ingredients:

    1 scallion, chopped
    1 carrot, grated or finely sliced
    ½ cucumber, finely sliced or chopped
    1 handful sprouts
    1 cup cooked brown rice
        tarragon vinegar or fresh lemon juice
        dash tamari
        freshly ground pepper to taste

Note: Any combination of vegetables that you desire may be used.

1. Combine all vegetables with rice and stir.
2. Sprinkle with tarragon vinegar or fresh lemon juice to taste.
3. Add a dash of tamari and a bit of freshly ground pepper.
4. Enjoy.

Serves 1

DINNER:

Poached Salmon with Yogurt-Dill Sauce

Ingredients:

> 2 5- or 6-ounce salmon fillets
>   juice of 1 lemon
> 2 bunches fresh dill—mince ⅓ cup, reserve sprigs for garnish
> 1 teaspoon Dijon mustard
> 1 cup plain yogurt

1. Place filleted salmon in wok.
2. Add cold water to cover the salmon by ¾ inch. Add juice of 1 lemon.
3. Turn heat to medium and bring to simmer. Cover and simmer gently over medium-low heat for 15 minutes. Turn heat off and let salmon sit in broth for 5 minutes.
4. Carefully remove salmon to warm plate.
5. Boil broth until reduced to ¾ cup.
6. Turn heat to low. Add dill and mustard.
7. Stir in yogurt. Heat through, but *do not boil*. Spoon sauce over salmon. Garnish with dill sprigs and serve. Reserve extra sauce for future use.

Note: Don't attempt this recipe if you are unable to find fresh salmon and fresh dill—they're essential. If you cannot find them, substitute any of the other fish dinners in the Thirty-Day Menu Plan.

Serves 2

Baked Potatoes

See Day #2 Dinner

Garden Salad

Prepare a salad of your favorite fresh vegetables.

DAY #

13
MENU

BREAKFAST:

Shredded Wheat Cereal with Fresh Fruit and Skim
Milk
Calories: 207

LUNCH:

Christopher's Tuna Delight in Pita Pocket
Calories: 194

DINNER:

Artichoke with Mustard Sauce
Twist of Lemon Chicken
Brown Rice with Mushrooms
Calories: 480
Day's Total Calories: 881

DAY #13 RECIPES

BREAKFAST:

Shredded Wheat Cereal with Fresh Fruit and Skim Milk

See Day #3 Breakfast.

LUNCH:

Christopher's Tuna Delight in Pita Pocket

See Day #6 Lunch.

DINNER:

Artichoke with Mustard Sauce

See Day #1 Dinner.

very good

I used frozen artichoke — cut back on mustard sauce ½ pg 56

Brown Rice with Mushrooms

good - needs most flavor

try adding pasta?

Ingredients:

oil for cooking
1 clove garlic, minced, or ½ teaspoon minced bottled garlic
1 teaspoon toasted sesame seeds
2 cups fresh mushrooms, brushed and sliced
2 cups cooked brown rice
freshly ground pepper

1. Heat wok.
2. Necklace with oil.
3. Add garlic, sesame seeds, and mushrooms. Stir fry 3 minutes.
4. Add rice. Stir fry till heated through.
5. Sprinkle with freshly ground pepper.
6. Remove to warmed serving heatproof bowl. Place in oven on low setting to keep warm while you prepare main course.

Serves 2

Twist of Lemon Chicken

O.K. not enough flavor

Ingredients:

1 pound boneless chicken breast
oil for cooking
1 clove garlic, minced, or ½ teaspoon minced bottled garlic
2 lemons (1 sliced into thin rounds; 1 for juice)
1 teaspoon dried parsley, or 2 tablespoons fresh finely minced parsley
freshly ground pepper to taste

1. Cut chicken into small strips.
2. Heat wok.
3. Necklace with oil, and add minced garlic, thinly sliced lemon, and chicken pieces.
4. While stir frying, add lemon juice, parsley, and pepper. Continue cooking until chicken is done, about 4 minutes.
5. Remove from wok and serve over Brown Rice with Mushrooms.

Serves 2

BREAKFAST:

Yogurt with Fresh Fruit and Wheat Germ
Calories: 204

LUNCH:

Tuna-Zucchini Burgers
Calories: 300

DINNER:

Chicken, Mussel, and Spinach Soup
Calories: 330
Day's Total Calories: 834

DAY #14 RECIPES

BREAKFAST:

Yogurt with Fresh Fruit and Wheat Germ

See Day #6 Breakfast

LUNCH:

Tuna-Zucchini Burgers

Ingredients:

½ cup firmly packed grated zucchini
½ onion, grated or finely minced
⅓ cup bulgur
¼ cup fresh mushrooms, finely minced
  juice of ½ lemon
2 tablespoons tamari
½ teaspoon hot chili oil, Tabasco, or cayenne pepper
⅛ cup fresh dill, or 1 teaspoon dried dill
½ 6½-ounce can tuna packed in water, drained and flaked
1 small egg, beaten
  oil for cooking
2 handfuls mung bean sprouts, well drained
  lettuce leaves for garnish

1. In a bowl, combine zucchini, onion, bulgur, mushrooms, lemon juice, 1 tablespoon tamari, chili oil, dill, and tuna. Let marinate for 20 minutes to 1 hour, until bulgur has absorbed all liquid and softened.
2. Mix in beaten egg.
3. Form into 4 small patties, the thinner the better.
4. Heat wok and necklace with oil.
5. Fry patties 2 at a time for 2 to 3 minutes on each side until browned and crusty. Remove from wok and keep warm
6. Add sprouts and 1 tablespoon tamari to wok, and stir fry 1 minute.
7. To serve, place large lettuce leaf on each plate. Put ½ the sprouts on each leaf, and top with 2 patties each.

Serves 2

Chicken, Mussel, and Spinach Soup

Ingredients:

    1 tablespoon oil
    2 teaspoons fresh ginger root, minced
    ½ cup scallions, thinly sliced
    1 clove garlic, minced
    ½ pound boneless chicken breast, cut into small strips
    4 cups chicken stock, canned without preservatives or
        homemade
    1 tablespoon tamari
    1 tablespoon tahini
    1 dozen mussels, well scrubbed
    1 pound fresh spinach, well scrubbed and trimmed

1. Heat wok over high heat.
2. Necklace with oil.
3. Add ginger, scallions, garlic, and chicken. Stir fry 1 minute.
4. Add chicken stock, tamari, and tahini. Bring to boil. Cover, heat, and simmer for 5 minutes.
5. Add mussels and bring to simmer. Cover and simmer gently for 8 to 10 minutes or until mussels open.
6. Stir in spinach. Turn off heat. Cover and let steep 1 minute.
7. Serve!

Serves 4

SHOPPING LIST WEEK #3

FRESH PRODUCE

Asparagus
Avocado
Beets
Broccoli
Carrots
Cauliflower
Celery
Cucumbers
Dill
Extra Vegetables for stir-frying
Fresh Fruit for Breakfast
Garlic
Green Peppers

Lemons
Mushrooms (large size)
Onions
Parsley
Red Cabbage
Red Pepper
Scallions
Snow peas (fresh or frozen)
Spaghetti Squash
Spinach
Sprouts
Tomatoes (or purée)

DAIRY

Butter
Cheddar Cheese
Cottage Cheese
Eggs
Milk

Mozzarella Cheese
Muenster Cheese (thin slices)
Parmesan Cheese
Yogurt

FRESH SEAFOOD AND POULTRY

Fish Fillet for Monday
Crabmeat for Tuesday
Frying Chicken for Thursday (to
feed 4)

Fish Fillet for Friday
Shrimp for Saturday

STAPLES FROM NATURAL-FOOD STORE

Bran
Bulgur (you should have it already)
Coconut (flaked or shredded, no sugar)
Miso Paste
Oyster Sauce
Raisins
Rice Cakes

Sesame Seeds
Tahini
Tamari
Tofu
Tomato Sauce
Vegetarian Bacon Bits
Wheat Germ
Whole-Wheat Bread
Whole-Wheat Pasta
Whole-Wheat Pita Pockets

STAPLES

Allspice (optional)
Basil
Crushed Red Pepper
Curry
Dijon Mustard
Mayonnaise
Olive Oil
Oregano
Paprika

Peanut Oil
Red Wine
Sesame Oil
Shredded Wheat Cereal
Tabasco
Tomato Paste
Tomato Purée or juice
Tuna (packed in water)
Worcestershire sauce

DAY #

15
MENU

BRUNCH:

Bloody Mary Eggs
1 Slice Whole-Wheat Toast
Calories: 250

DINNER:

Tofu Parmigiana
Tossed Garden Salad
Fresh Asparagus with Lemon
Calories: 540
Day's Total Calories: 790

DAY #15 RECIPES

BRUNCH:

Bloody Mary Eggs

Ingredients:

2 large eggs
5 ounces tomato purée or juice (purée is better)
½ cup celery, minced
2 teaspoons Worcestershire sauce
¼ teaspoon Tabasco, or to taste
1 tablespoon fresh snipped dill, or 1 teaspoon dried dill
1 teaspoon butter

1. Beat eggs until frothy, then beat in purée or juice.
2. Add celery, Worcestershire, Tabasco, and dill. Blend well.
3. Pour into 2 buttered ramekins or custard cups.
4. Dot with ½ teaspoon butter each.
5. Place on steamer rack set over simmering water in wok.
6. Cover and simmer 20 to 25 minutes until mixture is firm and knife inserted comes out clean.
7. Serve with 1 slice whole-wheat toast.

Serves 2

Note: If you get hungry during the day, snack on leftover Chicken, Mussel, and Spinach Soup. Also prepare bulgur for the week ahead.

Tofu Parmigiana

Ingredients:

    1½ pounds tofu (6 cakes)
      2 eggs
      1 tablespoon tamari
     ¾ cup wheat germ or bran
     ¾ cup grated Parmesan cheese
        oil for cooking
     ½ cup onions, sliced
      1 carrot, shredded
      2 cloves garlic, minced, or to taste
      1 cup fresh mushrooms, sliced
      2 cups tomatoes, seeded and diced, or 1 cup thick purée
      1 tablespoon fresh basil, chopped, or 1 teaspoon dried basil
      1 teaspoon oregano
     ¼ teaspoon crushed red pepper
        salt to taste
      8 thin slices low-fat mozzarella cheese
        cooked brown rice

1. Slice tofu cakes into 8 thin and equal slices.
2. In a shallow bowl, beat the eggs with the tamari until frothy and well blended.
3. Mix together wheat germ (or bran) and ¼ cup of the Parmesan in a dinner plate or pie plate.
4. Dip each tofu slice in egg, then in wheat germ and Parmesan mixture so that it is completely coated. Place coated tofu slices on a plate in a single layer and refrigerate while you prepare sauce.
5. Heat wok over high heat and necklace with oil.
6. Add onion, carrot, garlic, and mushrooms, and stir fry for several minutes until onions are translucent.
7. Add tomatoes, basil, oregano, and red pepper. Stir well, bring to the boil, reduce heat, and simmer (not boil) uncovered for 15 to 20 minutes or until vegetables are soft.
8. When sauce is done, add salt to taste. Transfer to bowl and set aside.
9. Wipe out wok. Heat clean wok over high heat and necklace with oil.

10. Fry sliced tofu two or three at a time, turning once, until golden.
11. Heat broiler. Cover bottom of shallow rectangular baking pan with a thin layer of sauce and sprinkle with ¼ cup of the Parmesan. Place browned tofu slices on sauce in a single layer. Top each tofu slice with a thin slice of mozzarella. Pour remaining sauce over and around tofu. Sprinkle remaining Parmesan over all.
12. Place under hot broiler until top is bubbly and beginning to brown and mozzarella is melted. Serve with cooked brown rice. Leftovers are delicious!

Serves 4

Garden Salad

Prepare a salad of your favorite fresh vegetables.

Fresh Asparagus with Lemon

See Day #5 Dinner.

DAY
16
MENU

BREAKFAST:

Shredded Wheat Cereal with Fresh Fruit and Skim
Milk
Calories: 207

LUNCH:

Leftover Tofu Parmigiana (or Tossed Garden Salad
with Rice Cake)
Calories: 200

DINNER:

Fresh Fish Fillets with Tahini Sauce
Tabouli Salad
Steamed Lemon Spinach
Calories: 286
Day's Total Calories: 693

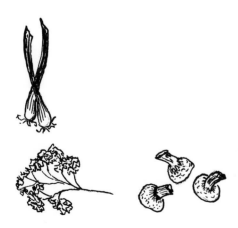

DAY #16 RECIPES

BREAKFAST:

Shredded Wheat Cereal with Fresh Fruit and Skim Milk

See Day #3 Breakfast.

LUNCH:

Leftover Tofu Parmigiana (or Tossed Garden Salad with Rice Cake)

See Day #3 Dinner.

DINNER:

Fresh Fish Fillets with Tahini Sauce, steamed, broiled, or grilled

See Day #1, 5, or 11 Dinner.

Tabouli Salad

Once you discover Tabouli Salad, it's a hard thing not to always have in your refrigerator. It's so easy and so good. It's made primarily from bulgur, which is sold in natural-food stores everywhere and costs about 55 cents a pound. That one pound will make two good-sized bowls of Tabouli. It's a perfect thing to take to work for lunch. It's also great as a substitute for coleslaw or potato salad at picnics, or all by itself as a light, nutritional meal. My gourmet friend Russell tells me he serves it hot, accompanying a main dinner course.

However you like it served, you'll probably consider Tabouli the diet food discovery of the decade!

Ingredients:

    4 cups water
    2 cups bulgur
    4 scallions
    2 tomatoes
    2 cucumbers
    1 bunch fresh parsley
    1 bunch fresh dill
      optional: a few leaves of fresh spearmint, if you have it, tastes great
    4 tablespoons tamari
    2 teaspoons toasted sesame seeds
      pepper to taste
    1 tablespoon oil (sesame is especially great here)
      juice of 2 lemons

1. Boil 4 cups water.
2. Pour over 2 cups bulgur in large bowl.
3. Allow to sit several hours until all water is absorbed.
4. Chop scallions.
5. Chop tomatoes and slice cucumber.
6. Chop parsley and dill (also spearmint, if using).
7. Add ingredients to bulgur and toss.
8. Add tamari, sesame seeds, pepper, and oil.
9. Pour in lemon juice and mix well.
10. Serve warm or refrigerate and serve as salad.

Yield: A bowl full!
(Leftovers are great for all week)

Steamed Spinach with Lemon

Ingredients:

1 pound fresh spinach
olive oil for cooking
1 clove garlic, minced, or ½ teaspoon minced bottled garlic
1 teaspoon toasted sesame seeds
salt and pepper to taste
juice of 1 lemon

1. Scrub spinach well to remove sand. Clip thick stalks.
2. Heat wok.
3. Necklace with oil.
4. Add garlic and sesame seeds. Stir fry 1 minute.
5. Add spinach, toss, and cover.
6. When spinach cooks down (about 3 minutes), sprinkle lightly with salt and pepper.
7. Pour lemon juice over and serve.

Serves 2

BREAKFAST:

Cottage Cheese with Fresh Fruit and Wheat Germ
Calories: 150

LUNCH:

Tabouli Salad
Calories: 206

DINNER:

Crab-Stuffed Mushrooms
Fresh Wokked Vegetables
Calories: 280
Day's Total Calories: 636

DAY #17 RECIPES

BREAKFAST:

Cottage Cheese with Fresh Fruit and Wheat Germ

See Day #1 Breakfast.

LUNCH:

Tabouli Salad

See Day #16 Dinner.

DINNER:

Crab-Stuffed Mushrooms

Ingredients:

½ pound crabmeat, canned or frozen
1 onion, finely minced
3 tablespoons fresh chopped parsley
  juice of one lemon
1 teaspoon tamari
1 cup water
6 large mushrooms, stems removed, rinsed and rubbed with oil
¾ cup shredded low-fat mozzarella cheese

1. Mix crabmeat with finely minced onion, parsley, lemon juice, and tamari.
2. Bring 1 cup water to boil in wok with steamer rack in place.
3. Stuff mushroom caps with crabmeat mixture and top with shredded cheese.
4. Arrange caps on steamer rack. Cover and steam until cheese melts.
5. Serve immediately with fresh wokked veggies.

Fresh Wokked Vegetables

Any of your favorite steamed or stir-fried vegetables.

Serves 2

DAY
18
MENU

BREAKFAST:

Yogurt with Fresh Fruit and Wheat Germ
Calories: 204

LUNCH:

Christopher's Tuna Delight in Whole-Wheat Pita
Pocket
Calories: 194

DINNER:

Pasta Primavera
Garden Salad
Calories: 420
Day's Total Calories: 818

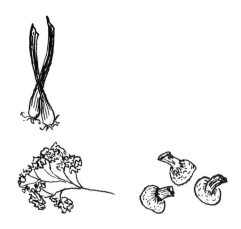

DAY #18 RECIPES

BREAKFAST:

Yogurt with Fresh Fruit and Wheat Germ

See Day #6 Breakfast.

LUNCH:

Christopher's Tuna Delight in Whole-Wheat Pita Pocket

See Day #6 Lunch.

DINNER:

Pasta Primavera

See Day #6 Dinner.

Garden Salad

Prepare a salad of your favorite fresh vegetables.

19
MENU

BREAKFAST:

Scallion and Mushroom Omelet with 1 Slice Whole-
Wheat Toast
Calories: 350

LUNCH:

Tabouli Salad (or Tossed Garden Salad with Rice
Cake)
Calories: 206

DINNER:

Chicken Cacciatore
Spaghetti Squash
Calories: 400
Day's Total Calories: 956

BREAKFAST:

Scallion and Mushroom Omelet

Ingredients:

4 eggs
1 tablespoon milk or water
salt and pepper to taste
pinch of basil
pinch of oregano
oil for cooking
1 cup sliced mushrooms
1 scallion, chopped
2 very thin slices muenster cheese, cut into strips

1. Beat eggs with milk or water, salt and pepper, basil and oregano.
2. Heat wok.
3. Necklace with oil.
4. Add mushrooms, scallion to wok. Stir fry 2 to 3 minutes.
5. Add eggs. Stir constantly. When eggs almost reach desired consistency, lay cheese strips over.
6. Sprinkle sides of wok with water to create steam. Cover.
7. Serve when cheese has melted with 1 slice whole-wheat toast per person.

Serves 2

LUNCH:

Tabouli Salad

See Day #16 Dinner.

(or Tossed Garden Salad with Rice Cake)

See Day #3 Dinner.

Chicken Cacciatore

Ingredients:

2 medium onions
1–2 green peppers
1 red pepper
3 cloves garlic
2 2-pound frying chickens, cut up
¼ cup olive oil
4 tomatoes
1½ cup tomato purée
¼ cup red wine
1½ teaspoon salt
⅛ teaspoon pepper
¼ teaspoon allspice (optional)
3 tablespoons tomato paste
1 teaspoon oregano
1 teaspoon basil

1. Chop onions, green and red peppers. Set aside.
2. Mince garlic. Set aside.
3. Rinse chicken. Pat dry.
4. Heat oil in wok.
5. Brown chicken pieces a few at a time and then place on plate.
6. Add onions, peppers, garlic to oil and brown lightly.
7. Add remaining ingredients and bring to boil; simmer 10 minutes uncovered.
8. Put chicken back into sauce and simmer covered 15 to 20 minutes.
9. Take off cover and simmer 10 minutes more. Serve.

Serves 4

Spaghetti Squash

When you live at the beach, a recurring theme, especially with the ladies, is pounds versus pasta. (Is it ever really worth it?) Well, once our summer house discovered spaghetti squash, we had the problem licked. It is a large yellow squash that contains a pulp of long spaghetti-like strings. Spaghetti squash tastes much like pasta—only it's not fattening at all! We think "pretend pasta" is the best, and it's as easy as 1, 2, 3!

Ingredients:

      1 large spaghetti squash
      1 quart tomato sauce, heated*
      Parmesan cheese

1. Place steamer rack in wok and pour boiling water beneath rack.
2. Split open squash and place both halves on rack. Cover wok and steam squash till tender (45 minutes to 1 hour).
3. When "spaghetti" pulls out of squash skin easily, it's ready. Pull out with fork, place in bowl, top with tomato sauce, and serve with grated Parmesan cheese.

Serves 2–4

*You can use extra sauce from Chicken Cacciatore.

20
MENU

BREAKFAST:

Shredded Wheat Cereal with
Fresh Fruit and Skim Milk
Calories: 207

LUNCH:

Avocado with Lettuce, Tomato, and Sprouts in Whole-
Wheat Pita Pocket
Calories: 279

DINNER:

Fresh Fish Fillets with Miso Sauce
Flo & Eddie's Sesame Mushrooms
Lanell's Stir-Fried Curried Cabbage
Calories: 262
Day's Total Calories: 769

DAY #20 RECIPES

BREAKFAST:

Shredded Wheat Cereal with Fresh Fruit and Skim Milk

See Day #3 Breakfast.

LUNCH:

Avocado with Lettuce, Tomato, and Sprouts in Whole-Wheat Pita Pocket

See Day #11 Lunch.

DINNER:

Fresh Fish Fillets with Miso Sauce

Ingredients:

> 1 teaspoon miso paste
> 1 tablespoon mayonnaise
> 2 6-ounce fresh fish fillets

1. Mix together miso and mayonnaise.
2. Brush lightly on both sides of fillet.
3. Steam, broil, or grill fillet till it flakes gently with fork.

Serves 2

Flo & Eddie's Sesame Mushrooms

Ingredients:

>   1 pound fresh mushrooms
>   sesame oil
>   2 cloves garlic, finely minced, or ½ teaspoon minced bottled garlic
>   3 tablespoons sesame seeds
>   1½ tablespoons fresh lemon juice

1. Wash mushrooms, remove stems from caps, and slice both.
2. Heat wok.
3. Necklace with oil.
4. Sauté garlic for 5 minutes.
5. Add mushrooms, sesame seeds, lemon juice, and salt and pepper.
6. Mix well. Simmer 10 minutes and serve.

Serves 2

This year a great gift came into my life and into the life of my friend Stanley. Her name is Lanell Doré. Stanley got a wife and I got a best friend all at once. You might have crossed paths with Lanell yourself. She does what they do best on American Airlines from New York City to Los Angeles, and has for the past fifteen years. As a matter of fact, they fondly recall that Stanley began simply as the man in Seat #51-H! Well, anyway, here's her recipe for Curried Cabbage. It's so great you might forget it's almost calorie-free.

Lanell's Stir-Fried Curried Cabbage

Ingredients:

>   sesame oil for cooking
>   1 head red cabbage, sliced
>   1 handful raisins
>   1 tablespoon coconut, flaked or shredded
>   1 tablespoon vegetarian bacon bits
>   1 teaspoon curry, or to taste
>   1–2 tablespoons tamari

1. Heat wok.
2. Necklace with oil.
3. Add all ingredients, toss, and cover. Cook over low heat.
4. Stir and serve when cabbage is tender.

Serves 2

BREAKFAST:

Cottage Cheese with Fresh Fruit and Wheat Germ
Calories: 150

LUNCH:

California Cauliflower
Calories: 250

DINNER:

Shrimp and Broccoli in Oyster Sauce with cooked rice
Calories: 400
Day's Total Calories: 800

DAY #21 RECIPES

BREAKFAST:

Cottage Cheese with Fresh Fruit and Wheat Germ

See Day #1 Breakfast.

LUNCH:

California Cauliflower

This recipe is dedicated to my favorite place in the world—California!

Ingredients:

> oil for cooking
> 1 head cauliflower, decored and cut into thin, small pieces
> 1 red pepper, chopped
> 1 scallion, chopped
> 1 tablespoon sesame seeds
> salt and pepper to taste
> pinch of basil
> ¾ cup shredded cheddar cheese

1. Heat wok.
2. Necklace with oil.
3. Add cauliflower pieces. Stir fry 4 to 5 minutes or till tender.
4. Add red pepper, scallion, sesame seeds, salt and pepper, and basil. Stir fry till tender.
5. Sprinkle with cheese. Sprinkle water around side of wok to create steam. Cover.
6. When cheese is melted, serve.

Serves 2

DINNER:

Shrimp* and Broccoli in Oyster Sauce

Ingredients:

oregon olive oil

oil for cooking - *oregon olive oil*

4-6
1–2 cloves garlic, minced, or ½ teaspoon minced bottled garlic

) large frozen pkg.
1 small head broccoli, cut into thin small pieces

1 red pepper, chopped

1 small onion, chopped

) large
1 pound fresh shrimp, shelled (or frozen shrimp, defrosted)

2 tablespoons oyster sauce

1 tablespoon water

hot cooked rice

1. Heat wok.
2. Necklace with oil.
3. Add garlic. Stir fry 30 seconds.
4. Add broccoli. Stir fry 4 to 5 minutes or until crisp-tender. Remove to plate.
5. Add red pepper, onion to wok. Stir fry 5 minutes.
6. Add shrimp. Stir fry 3 minutes till pink. Do not overcook.
7. Add broccoli and oyster sauce and water to wok. Stir to combine. Heat through.
8. Serve over hot cooked rice.

*Chicken breasts cut into strips can be substituted for shrimp.

SHOPPING LIST WEEK #4

FRESH PRODUCE

Asparagus (if available)	Lemons
Broccoli	Lettuce
Cabbage	Mushrooms
Carrots	Onions
Cauliflower	Parsley
Celery	Potatoes (Idaho or sweet)
Eggplant	Red Pepper
Fennel	Scallions
Fresh Basil (if possible)	Spinach
Fresh Fruit for Breakfast	Sprouts
Garlic	Strawberries
Ginger Root	Tomatoes
Grapefruit	Turnips
Green Pepper	Zucchini

DAIRY

Cheddar Cheese	Goat Cheese (optional)
Cottage Cheese	Parmesan Cheese
Eggs	Yogurt

FRESH SEAFOOD AND POULTRY

Fresh Mussels for Friday
Boneless Breasts of Chicken for
Tuesday

Roasting Chicken for Sunday
Lobster Pieces (fresh, canned, or
frozen) for Thursday

STAPLES FROM NATURAL-FOOD STORE

Almonds
Brown Rice
Honey
Rice Cakes
Sesame Oil
Sesame Seeds
Spaghetti Sauce

Tamari
Tofu
Wheat Germ
Whole-Wheat Bread
Whole-Wheat English Muffins
Whole-Wheat Pasta
Whole-Wheat Pita Pockets

STAPLES

Baking Powder
Basil
Bay Leaves
Canned Tomato Sauce
Caraway Seeds
Cashews
Cayenne Pepper
Crushed Red Pepper
Dijon Mustard
Gin (optional)
Mayonnaise
Olive Oil
Oregano
Oyster Sauce

Peanut Oil
Saffron (if available)
Sesame Oil
Shredded Wheat Cereal
Tarragon (dried)
Tarragon Vinegar
Thyme (dried)
Tuna (packed in water)
Unbleached White Flour
Vanilla
Vermouth (optional)
Walnuts
White wine

DAY #
22
MENU

BRUNCH:

Fresh Grapefruit Half
Zucchini and Eggs
with Brown Rice
Calories: 320

DINNER:

Roast Lemon Chicken
Baked Potato
Martinied Eggplant
Calories: 630
Day's Total Calories: 950

DAY #22 RECIPES

BRUNCH:

Fresh Grapefruit Half
Zucchini and Eggs with Brown Rice

See Day #4 Breakfast.

DINNER:

Roast Lemon Chicken, Baked Potato

See Day #2 Dinner.

Martinied Eggplant

Ingredients:

1 eggplant, peeled
1 green pepper
1 onion
  oil for cooking
1 tablespoon sesame seeds
1 jigger gin
  salt and pepper to taste
½ teaspoon white vermouth

1. Wash eggplant and cut into 1-inch cubes. Set aside.
2. Wash green pepper and cut into 1-inch strips. Set aside.
3. Peel onion and slice. Set aside.
4. Heat wok.
5. Necklace with oil.
6. Add sesame seeds, onion, and green pepper. Toss for 3 minutes.
7. Add eggplant. Toss and cover.
8. Stir fry for 5 minutes over medium heat. Then simmer over low heat for 20 minutes.
9. Add gin, raise heat, stir constantly. Add salt and pepper to taste, and vermouth.
10. When veggies are tender, enjoy your martini.

2–4 Servings

Note: Prepare rice and miso soup for this week.

BREAKFAST:

Yogurt with Fresh Fruit and Wheat Germ
Calories: 204

LUNCH:

Stanley's Chunky Chicken Salad in
Whole-Wheat Pita Pocket
Calories: 288

DINNER:

Lady A's Blue Plate Special
Calories: 370
Day's Total Calories: 862

DAY #23 RECIPES

BREAKFAST:

Yogurt with Fresh Fruit and Wheat Germ

See Day #6 Breakfast.

LUNCH:

Stanley's Chunky Chicken Salad in Whole-Wheat Pita Pocket

See Day #3 Lunch.

Lady A's Blue Plate Special

Every cook has an old standby, a familiar friend of a recipe that's a pleasure to fall back on. This one has become mine. I eat it often and with countless variations. It never disappoints—it's always inexpensive, easy, and delicious.

Ingredients:

            oil for cooking
    3 carrots, shredded
    1 head broccoli or cauliflower, chopped into small pieces
    1 medium-sized onion, minced
    4 large fresh mushrooms, sliced
    4 cups cooked brown rice, preferably cold
    ¾ cup walnut pieces
            tamari to taste
    1 tablespoon toasted sesame seeds

1. Heat wok.
2. Necklace with oil.
3. Add veggies and stir fry till almost tender.
4. Add rice and nuts and sprinkle with tamari. Stir well.
5. Add sesame seeds.
6. Stir till rice is heated and then serve.

Note: Variations can include fresh chopped ginger root, tofu, and any assortment of available seasonal vegetables.

Serves 2

BREAKFAST:

Shredded Wheat Cereal with Fresh Fruit and Skim
Milk
Calories: 207

LUNCH:

Tofu Salad Delight in Whole-Wheat Pita Pocket
Calories: 229

DINNER:

Tarragon Chicken with Brown Rice
Broccoli in Oyster Sauce
Calories: 400
Day's Total Calories: 836

DAY #24 RECIPES

BREAKFAST:

Shredded Wheat Cereal with Fresh Fruit and Skim Milk

See Day #3 Breakfast.

LUNCH:

Tofu Salad Delight in Whole-Wheat Pita Pocket

See Day #5 Lunch.

DINNER:

Tarragon Chicken with Brown Rice

If I had to pick a couple to be stranded with anywhere in the world, I would pick Eddie and Eileen Friedman. The primary reason is that wherever they are, they always have a great time. They are one of those blessed couples who maintain their sense of fun and good humor throughout all of life's changing scenes, and who are genuinely interested in everything there is to learn. When we met, food was an insignificant part of their life-style. They worked incredibly long hours at their film-editing company, DJM, all week long, and on the weekends they played hard on their beautiful boat, *Eddie's Mink*. Well, after a few outings together on the boat, Eileen and Eddie agreed to experiment: Instead of preparing the regular deck barbecue, we tried out wokked food to see how it went over with family and friends. As usual, people flipped over the fare, and Eileen could not believe how easy it was to prepare. That was it. The next step was turning their town house kitchen into a real Wokmaster's studio. I called First Stop Housewares, my favorite housewares store on 2nd Ave. at 54th St. in New York City, and had them deliver everything from a rice pot to a cutting board—all that she would need.

Well, Eileen's a bona fide Wokmaster now. In fact, her diet is exclusively wok food and sushi, and her body never looked better. Eddie says both the food and the figure have won his heart. As a very special thank you for all the wonderful fun we've had together, I've created this next dish in their honor.

Ingredients:

oil for cooking
2 pounds boneless chicken breast, diced
½ teaspoon dried tarragon
½ cup walnuts
2 scallions, chopped
2 carrots, sliced finely
2 tablespoons tarragon vinegar, or to taste
cooked brown rice

1. Heat wok.
2. Necklace with oil.
3. Stir fry chicken with tarragon and walnuts till chicken is white. Remove to plate.
4. Add scallions and carrots to wok. Stir fry till crisp-tender.
5. Add chicken mixture to vegetables in wok. Stir together.
6. Splash with vinegar. Stir and serve over rice.

Serves 2

Broccoli in Oyster Sauce

Ingredients:

1 small head broccoli
oil for cooking
1 clove garlic, minced, or ½ teaspoon minced bottled garlic
2 tablespoons oyster sauce, or to taste
1 tablespoon water

1. Cut broccoli into small, thin flowerets and pieces.
2. Heat wok.
3. Necklace with oil.
4. Add garlic, stir fry 1 minute or until golden.
5. Add broccoli, toss, and stir fry.
6. Add oyster sauce and water. Toss again.
7. When broccoli is crisp-tender, serve, or place in heatproof bowl in warm oven to keep hot while you prepare main course.

Serves 2

BREAKFAST:

Cottage Cheese with Fresh Fruit and Wheat Germ
Calories: 150

LUNCH:

Christopher's Tuna Delight in Whole-Wheat Pita
Pocket with Lettuce, Tomato, and Sprouts
Calories: 194

DINNER:

Vegetarian Feast for Two
Calories: 400
Day's Total Calories: 744

DAY #25 RECIPES

BREAKFAST:

Cottage Cheese with Fresh Fruit and Wheat Germ

See Day #1 Breakfast.

LUNCH:

Christopher's Tuna Delight in Whole-Wheat Pita Pocket

See Day #6 Lunch.

Vegetarian Feast
for Two

Ingredients:

    oil for cooking
1 large clove garlic, minced, or ½ teaspoon minced, bottled garlic
1 tablespoon sesame seeds
1 small head broccoli, cut into small pieces
½ pound mushrooms, sliced
1 red pepper, diced
1 onion or 2 scallions, chopped
3 cups cooked brown rice
    tamari to taste
    fresh ground pepper or cayenne pepper
½ cup shredded cheddar cheese

1. Heat wok.
2. Necklace with oil.
3. Add garlic and sesame seeds. Stir fry 30 seconds.
4. Add broccoli. Stir fry 3 to 5 minutes till crisp-tender. Remove to plate.
5. Add mushrooms, red pepper, and onion. Stir fry 3 to 5 minutes.
6. Add rice and broccoli to wok. Stir fry and mix together.
7. Season with tamari and pepper or cayenne.
8. Sprinkle cheese over rice. Sprinkle sides of wok with water to create steam.
9. When cheese is melted, serve.

Serves 2

DAY #
26
MENU

BREAKFAST:

Fresh Grapefruit Half
Scallioned Sesame Eggs, 1 Slice Whole-Wheat Toast
Calories: 294

LUNCH:

Tossed Garden Salad with Rice Cake
Calories: 200

DINNER:

Wokked Lobster
Calories: 435
Day's Total Calories: 929

DAY #26 RECIPES

BREAKFAST:

Fresh Grapefruit Half
Scallioned Sesame Eggs

See Day #8 Brunch.

LUNCH:

Tossed Garden Salad
with Rice Cake

See Day #4 Lunch.

Imagine a man as good in the kitchen as he is on Wall Street and you will have begun to imagine Bruce Dorfman.

Bruce is a Wall Street economic consultant and the author, along with Ira Cobleigh, of *The Dowbeaters* and *The Roaring '80's on Wall Street* (Macmillan). We met at a party sometime back when in the midst of casual party talk both of us admitted to being in the crazy final week of closing out our second books. The week before a manuscript is due is usually filled with re-writes, research, typists, and editors. Our first "date" was hardly a social affair, as we sat in my living room with thousands of sheets of paper around us bouncing ideas off each other and rather frantically preparing the final manuscripts for submission. Well, the books turned out great—and so did we. I learned an enormous amount about Wall Street—and Bruce became a Wokmaster!

Wokked Lobster

Ingredients:

sesame oil for cooking

2–3 cups raw lobster meat pieces (either fresh, canned, or frozen; if using frozen lobster tails, figure 2 small tails per person)

2 slices fresh ginger root, minced

½ pound asparagus, sliced diagonally

3 scallions, chopped

½ cup cashews or cashew pieces

1½ cups broccoli pieces, cut finely

tamari to taste

cooked brown rice

1. Heat wok.
2. Necklace with sesame oil.
3. Stir fry lobster pieces and ginger root for 2 to 3 minutes or until lobster pieces are white and firm. Remove to plate.
4. Add asparagus, scallions, cashews, and broccoli to wok. Stir fry till tender (3 to 5 minutes).
5. Return lobster and ginger to wok.
6. Sprinkle with tamari to taste (about 1 to 2 tablespoons) and toss.
7. Serve immediately over brown rice.

Serves 2

BREAKFAST:

Yogurt with Fresh Fruit and Wheat Germ
Calories: 204

LUNCH:

Tofu Salad Delight in Pita Pocket with Sprouts
Calories: 159

DINNER:

Pasta with Broccoli, Mussels, and Garlic
Calories: 325
Day's Total Calories: 688

DAY #27 RECIPES

BREAKFAST:

Yogurt with Fresh Fruit and Wheat Germ

See Day #6 Breakfast.

LUNCH:

Tofu Salad Delight in Pita Pocket with Sprouts

See Day #5 Lunch.

Pasta with Broccoli, Mussels, and Garlic

Ingredients:

1 small head fresh broccoli (or ½ large head)
1 dozen fresh mussels in shell
¾ pound whole grain pasta
  olive oil for cooking
3–4 large cloves fresh garlic, minced, or 2 teaspoons minced bottled garlic
  salt and pepper
½ teaspoon oregano
1 quart spaghetti sauce (your favorite recipe or bottled)

1. Cut broccoli into small bite-sized pieces. Set aside.
2. Scrub mussels well; they're sandy. Discard any with open shells.
3. Put salted water to boil for pasta. Cook al dente according to directions.
4. Heat wok.
5. Necklace with oil.
6. Add garlic. Stir fry 30 seconds.
7. Add broccoli pieces. Stir fry 3 to 5 minutes or until crisp-tender. Sprinkle with salt, pepper, oregano.
8. Heat sauce in large pot.
9. Add mussels and cook till mussels open.
10. Drain pasta when ready. Toss with sauce.
11. Top with garlic and broccoli and mussels in shell.
12. Sprinkle with Parmesan cheese and serve.

Serves 2–3

DAY #

28
MENU

BREAKFAST:

Eggs Alaska
Calories: 350

LUNCH:

The Funny Boys Spinach Special
Calories: 120

DINNER:

Squash and Potatoes Italiano
Garden Salad
Calories: 400
Day's Total Calories: 870

DAY #28 RECIPES

BREAKFAST:

Eggs Alaska

Ingredients:

>   1 large onion, peeled
>   1 dozen mushrooms, brushed and stalks trimmed
>   4 ounces cheddar cheese
>   oil for cooking
>   ½ teaspoon salt
>   pepper to taste
>   ½ teaspoon dried basil
>   4 eggs, separated carefully—each yolk set aside singularly
>   2 whole-wheat English muffins

 1. Preheat oven to 450°F.
 2. Slice onion and mushrooms. Set aside.
 3. Shred cheese. Set aside.
 4. Heat wok.
 5. Necklace with oil.
 6. Stir fry onion and mushrooms until golden.
 7. Season with ¼ teaspoon salt, pepper, and basil. Turn off heat.
 8. With electric mixer, beat egg whites till fluffy.
 9. Add remaining salt and beat till stiff peaks form.
10. Fold in shredded cheese.
11. To assemble: Divide vegetable mixture among muffin halves. Pile egg white mixture on top of each. Make an indentation in whites to serve as a nest for a yolk. Put a yolk in each nest.
12. Bake 7 to 10 minutes, or until yolks set. Serve.

Serves 2

The Funny Boys Spinach Special

Chances are if you watch television or visit comedy clubs, you've enjoyed the company of "The Funny Boys." Based in Los Angeles and New York, they tour the country bringing the joy of laughter wherever they go. Of course, by knowing The Funny Boys, I've had to endure all sorts of wok jokes but it's worth it—they do keep me laughing. They also join me in the kitchen occasionally. This is one of their favorites.

Ingredients:

    oil for cooking
1 clove garlic, minced, or ½ teaspoon bottled, minced garlic
½ pound mushrooms
½ cup walnuts, coarsely chopped
1 pound spinach, washed carefully (it's sandy) and stems clipped
    salt and pepper
2 tablespoons goat cheese (optional)

1. Heat wok.
2. Necklace with oil.
3. Add garlic. Stir fry 30 seconds.
4. Add mushrooms and nuts. Stir fry 2 minutes.
5. Add spinach and toss.
6. Sprinkle with salt and pepper to taste. Cover.
7. When spinach is tender (about 3 minutes), stir in goat cheese, if using, and serve.

Serves 1–2

DINNER:

Squash and Potatoes Italiano

This is another dish whose origin goes back far with me. I first tried making it in college when, in the face of dormitory food, I got myself a hot plate. My roommate, Mary, was the first of many to wrinkle her nose at the sound of it and then proceed to wolf it down after a timid taste. Years after college, it became the dish I always brought to those "everybody bring something" feasts that happen occasionally. It was the perfect choice to bring a lot of, since it is inexpensive, and easy to make and transport. It also happens to be absolutely delicious. Besides, no one else *ever* brought it, and whether it was a Yoga ashram or a Tupperware party, it was a sure hit!

It's actually amazingly convenient to make for a lot of people. One night I remember making it in the country for dinner for myself. Just as I was cutting up the squash, a car pulled up with a few friends. We all decided we were starving, so I just kept cutting up more squash. Not five minutes later, I heard the rumble of tires on the gravel again. Sure enough, a little green van pulled up filled with fine, familiar faces who, of course, were also starved. It was the perfect dish to have been making. I just cut up more of everything, filled the wok to capacity, and within about a half hour twelve people sat down to dinner.

Ingredients:

    1 clove garlic
    1 small onion
  4–5 zucchini or yellow squash
  3–4 potatoes
      oil for cooking
    1 tablespoon sesame seeds
    2 small cans tomato sauce
      dash white wine
      pinch dried oregano
      salt and pepper to taste
  ½ cup grated Parmesan cheese

1. Mince garlic and set aside.
2. Peel and chop onion and set aside.
3. Wash zucchini or squash, cut into chunks, and set aside.
4. Wash potatoes well and cut into 1-inch cubes. Set aside.
5. Heat wok.
6. Necklace with oil.
7. Add garlic, sesame seeds, and onion; stir fry until golden.
8. Add tomato sauce and wine; simmer 5 minutes.
9. Add zucchini or squash and cook 5 minutes.
10. Add potatoes, oregano, salt, and pepper; stir and cover.
11. When potatoes are tender, it's ready.
12. Sprinkle heavily with Parmesan cheese and serve.

Serves 2

Garden Salad

Prepare a salad of your favorite fresh vegetables.

29
MENU

BRUNCH:

Strawberry Pancakes with Fresh Berry Sauce
Calories: 400

DINNER:

Bouillabaisse
Calories: 350
Day's Total Calories: 750

DAY #29 RECIPES

BRUNCH:

Strawberry Pancakes with Fresh Berry Sauce

Ingredients:

1 egg
1 teaspoon oil
1 cup milk
¾ cup unbleached white flour
½ teaspoon salt
½ teaspoon baking powder
½ teaspoon vanilla
½ pint strawberries (or blueberries), rinsed, hulled, and halved
1 teaspoon honey
oil for cooking

Sauce Ingredients:

⅛ cup water
½ cup honey
½ pint strawberries

1. In blender add egg, oil, and milk. Process till blended or beat by hand.
2. Add flour, salt, baking powder, and vanilla. Process till blended or beat.
3. Add berries and honey. Process 5 seconds or mix by hand.
4. Preheat oven to 200°F. Heat 1 tablespoon oil in cast-iron skillet or griddle.
5. Pour batter to form pancakes. Flip when edges begin to bubble.
6. Place in warm oven to keep hot.

To Make Berry Sauce:

1. In small saucepan, combine water and honey, and bring to boil over medium heat. Boil 3 minutes.
2. Place strawberries in blender. Process, just for an instant, while pouring honey-water mixture in through hole in cover of blender. Serve over pancakes. Store in refrigerator.

Serves 2

DINNER:

Bouillabaisse

Ingredients:

2 tablespoons oil
1 cup onion, chopped
1 cup celery, chopped, including leaves
2 cloves garlic, minced, or to taste
½ cup carrots, sliced
1 small bulb fennel, sliced
4 small turnips, sliced
3 tomatoes, chopped
3 cups water, fish broth, or clam juice
2 cups dry white wine
½ teaspoon salt, or to taste
½ teaspoon thyme
pinch saffron (optional)
¼ teaspoon crushed red pepper
1 bay leaf
2 pounds lean fish fillets cut into chunks (cod, haddock, snapper, perch, sea bass, sea trout, weakfish, flounder, sole, etc. Use all one kind or mix several different kinds.)
1½–2 dozen clams or mussels, well scrubbed
juice and grated rind of 1 lemon, or more to taste

1. Heat wok over high heat and necklace with oil.
2. When oil is hot but not smoking, add chopped onion, chopped celery, and minced garlic. Stir fry several minutes until golden.
3. Add sliced carrots, fennel, and turnips, and stir to coat with oil.
4. Add chopped tomatoes, water (or fish broth or clam juice), wine, salt, thyme, saffron, crushed red pepper, and bay leaf. Bring to boil. Simmer over low heat, covered, for about 20 minutes.
5. Add fish pieces, clams or mussels, lemon juice, and rind. Cover and simmer gently another 15 minutes, or until fish is done and clams or mussels have opened.
6. To serve, place several pieces of fish and clams in each bowl, along with some of the vegetables. Ladle hot broth over fish and vegetables.

Serves 4

30
MENU

BREAKFAST:

Shredded Wheat Cereal with Fresh Fruit and Skim
Milk
Calories: 207

LUNCH:

Tossed Garden Salad with Rice Cake
Calories: 200

DINNER:

Sesame Almond Chicken
Brown Rice
Caraway Cabbage
Calories: 420
Day's Total Calories: 827

DAY #30 RECIPES

BREAKFAST:

Shredded Wheat Cereal with Fresh Fruit and Skim Milk

See Day #3 Breakfast.

LUNCH:

Tossed Garden Salad with Rice Cake

See Day #3 Dinner.

DINNER:

Sesame Almond Chicken

Ingredients:

      peanut oil for cooking
- ¼ cup almonds
- 2 scallions, chopped
- ½ pound mushrooms, sliced
- 1 teaspoon sesame oil
- 2 boneless breasts of chicken, cut into 2-inch strips
- 1 tablespoon sesame seeds
- 1–2 tablespoons tamari
  hot cooked rice

1. Heat wok.
2. Necklace with peanut oil.
3. Add almonds and scallions, and stir fry 1 minute.
4. Add mushrooms. Stir fry 3 minutes.
5. Remove to plate.
6. Add sesame oil to wok. Add chicken pieces and sesame seeds. Stir fry till chicken turns white, about 4 to 5 minutes.
7. Return vegetables to wok. Add tamari and stir.
8. Serve over hot cooked rice.

Serves 2

Caraway Cabbage

Ingredients:

      oil for cooking
1 clove garlic, or ½ teaspoon minced bottled garlic
1 head cabbage, sliced
1 tablespoon caraway seed
1 teaspoon curry, or to taste
      salt and pepper to taste
2 tablespoons tarragon vinegar

1. Heat wok.
2. Necklace with oil.
3. Add garlic, and stir fry 1 minute.
4. Add cabbage and caraway. Toss and season with curry, salt, and pepper.
5. When cabbage is tender, splash with vinegar and serve.

Serves 2

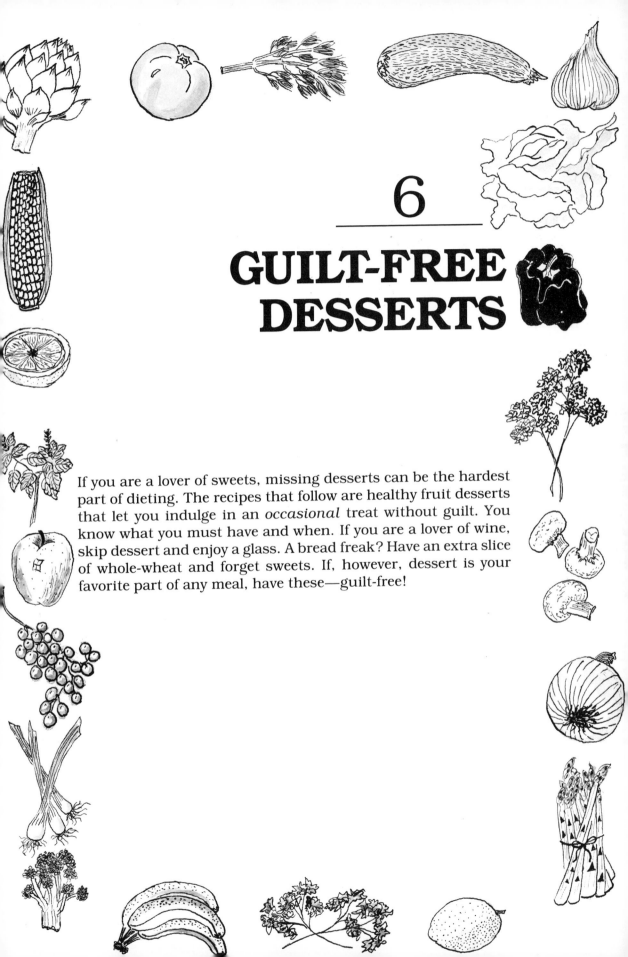

6

GUILT-FREE DESSERTS

If you are a lover of sweets, missing desserts can be the hardest part of dieting. The recipes that follow are healthy fruit desserts that let you indulge in an *occasional* treat without guilt. You know what you must have and when. If you are a lover of wine, skip dessert and enjoy a glass. A bread freak? Have an extra slice of whole-wheat and forget sweets. If, however, dessert is your favorite part of any meal, have these—guilt-free!

Wokked Ambrosia

Ingredients:

2 tablespoons unsalted butter
1 cup fresh coconut, or unsweetened packaged, grated
2 cups fresh grapefruit sections
1 large apple, cored and diced
1 large banana, peeled and sliced
½ cup dates, pitted and sliced
¼ teaspoon allspice
2 tablespoons honey

1. Melt butter in wok over medium heat.
2. Add coconut. Toss to coat with butter and stir fry briskly until coconut is golden and toasted.
3. Add remaining ingredients. Toss to blend well.
4. Cover wok and steam 1 to 2 minutes or until heated through.

Serves 4

Spiced Pears

Ingredients:

2 cups dry red wine
1 cup apple juice
½ cup honey
1 bay leaf
8 black peppercorns
4 whole cloves
1 2-inch stick cinnamon
1 1-inch piece vanilla bean
4 large firm ripe pears, halved, cored, and peeled

1. Place all ingredients except pears in wok. Bring to boil over high heat, and boil uncovered 3 to 4 minutes.
2. Add pears. Reduce heat to medium and simmer uncovered 15 minutes or until pears are tender but not mushy.
3. Carefully remove pears to a large bowl.
4. Over high heat boil liquid remaining in wok until reduced to 2 cups. Strain liquid over pears in bowl. Cool.
5. Serve pear halves with a bit of the liquid spooned over them.

Serves 4

Integral Yoga Institute's Chunky Apple Sauce

Ingredients:

8–10 apples, sliced in ½-inch chunks
1 ripe banana, cut in pieces
½ cup water
½ cup raisins
1 teaspoon cinnamon, or to taste
1 tablespoon wheat germ
¼ teaspoon nutmeg

1. Place apple chunks and banana pieces in wok with water.
2. Cook over low heat till apples start to soften, about 8 to 10 minutes.
3. Add raisins, cinnamon, wheat germ, and nutmeg and stir.
4. Cook 5 more minutes.
5. Serve warm or cold.

Serves 6

Yummy Brown Rice Pudding

Ingredients:

  2 eggs, lightly beaten
  1 cup apple juice
  ½ cup milk
  1½ tablespoons honey, or to taste
  1 teaspoon vanilla
  1 teaspoon fresh lemon juice
  ½ teaspoon grated orange peel
  1 tablespoon coconut, flaked or shredded
  ⅛ teaspoon salt
  ½ teaspoon cinnamon
  ¼ teaspoon nutmeg
  ¼ cup raisins or currants
  2 cups cooked brown rice
    yogurt or cottage cheese (optional)

1. Mix eggs with apple juice, milk, honey, vanilla, lemon juice, orange peel, coconut, salt, cinnamon, and nutmeg.
2. Add raisins or currants and rice. Mix again.
3. Place in slightly oiled baking dish.
4. Place on steam rack in wok over boiling water.
5. Cover and steam 45 minutes.
6. Serve warm or cool with yogurt or cottage cheese.

Serves 4

Pears Ricotta

Ingredients:

  4 very ripe unblemished pears
  ¼ cup fresh lemon juice
  ½ cup ricotta
  1 tablespoon honey
  1 tablespoon golden raisins, chopped
  2 dates, pitted and chopped
  1 teaspoon crystallized ginger, chopped very fine (optional)
  ⅛ teaspoon ground cloves
  2–3 tablespoons toasted slivered almonds

1. Peel pears, slice them in half lengthwise, and remove cores with a melon baller or tablespoon. Dip pear halves in lemon juice to prevent discoloration. Keep halves of the same pear together.
2. Combine ricotta, honey, raisins, dates, ginger, and cloves.
3. Place about 2 tablespoons of the ricotta mixture in a pear half. Cover with matching pear half. Fill remaining pears.
4. Arrange on individual serving plates and sprinkle with toasted almonds.

Serves 4

Baked Apples for Two

Ingredients:

         2 large apples
       ⅛ teaspoon salt
¼–½ cup raisins (or currants or chopped dates)
         2 tablespoons coconut
       ½ teaspoon cinnamon
       ⅛ teaspoon nutmeg
       1 teaspoon wheat germ
       ½ cup apple juice
         2 scoops cottage cheese

1. Preheat oven to 350°F.
2. Cut tops off apples and core. Do not peel. Rub small amount of salt into each hollow.
3. Chop apple tops and mix with raisins, coconut, cinnamon, nutmeg, and wheat germ.
4. Stuff mixture into apples.
5. Place apples in baking dish and add juice to bottom of dish.
6. Cover and bake 50 minutes or until tender.
7. Serve warm with cottage cheese.

Serves 2

Strawberry Coconut Cheese Pie

Ingredients:

1 tablespoon unflavored gelatin
¼ cup cold water
¼ cup hot water
1 teaspoon grated orange peel (also called zest)
1 tablespoon honey
2 cups cottage cheese
1 tablespoon wheat germ
1 cup unsweetened fruit juice
1 cup freshly grated coconut
 oiled 9-inch glass pie plate
1 cup fresh halved strawberries (or any other fresh fruit)

1. Stir gelatin into cold water to soften.
2. Pour in hot water and stir until dissolved.
3. Add grated orange peel (zest), honey, wheat germ, and juice.
4. Beat cottage cheese to creamy consistency in blender or with hand mixer, and fold into gelatin mixture.
5. Press coconut into the oiled pie plate, reserving some for top.
6. Pour in cheese mixture.
7. Garnish with strawberries and additional coconut.

Serves 6–8

Yogurt Popsicles

Ingredients:

½ cup plain yogurt
½ cup water
2 teaspoons nonfat dry milk
½ cup thawed unsweetened apple juice concentrate

1. Blend or beat all ingredients together at low speed.
2. Freeze in plastic popsicle containers.

Serves 3

(Only 40 calories each!)

Fruit Popsicles

Ingredients:

1 cup fresh berries
1 cup water
1 cup thawed unsweetened apple juice concentrate
1 teaspoon lemon juice

1. Purée all ingredients in blender or food processor.
2. Freeze in plastic popsicle containers.

Serves 6

Regis Philbin's Amaretto Poached Pears with Cottage Cheese

An elegant, simple dessert that is perfect for company as well as your diet! This one was created for TV host Regis Philbin, one of the most creative men in the business.

Ingredients

    1 large pear
    2 cups white grape juice (available in health food stores) *or* 2 cups white wine
    2 tablespoons amaretto (optional)
    ½ teaspoon cinnamon
    ¼ cup raisins
    2 tablespoons shredded coconut
    4 tablespoons slivered almonds
    2 scoops cottage cheese
    1 teaspoon wheat germ

1. Slice pear lengthwise; do not peel or remove stem.
2. Put juice or wine in wok, bring to boil, reduce heat to simmer.
3. Set pear in wok. Sprinkle with amaretto, cinnamon, raisins, coconut, and almonds.
4. Cover and simmer until tender when pierced with fork (about 10 minutes).
5. Lift out onto dessert plates. Boil remaining liquid 3 minutes longer.
6. Top each pear half with a scoop of cottage cheese, pour a bit of sauce over. Sprinkle with wheat germ. Enjoy. Remaining sauce is an ideal drink—hot or cold!

Serves 2

Annie's Apricot Tofu Pie

You won't believe this one—it tastes like *cheesecake* but it's low calorie. It's my all-time favorite healthy dessert. Don't let the length of the recipe scare you—it's easy to make!

Ingredients:

Crust:

> 1½ cups of your favorite granola
> ¼ cup apple cider
> ¼ teaspoon almond extract

Tofu Filling:

> ⅓ cup water
> 2 tablespoons oil or 1 tablespoon tahini
> 2 teaspoons vanilla extract
> ⅓ cup maple syrup (check the label for sugar)
> 1 pound tofu, crumbled
> juice of 1 lemon
> pinch of salt

Topping:

> ¼ cup unsulphured dried apricots
> 1¾ cups apple cider
> dash of cinnamon
> 1 vanilla bean (split)
> 1 tablespoon kuzo (available in health food stores)

1. Preheat oven to 375°F.
2. Add granola to blender or food processor and process until coarse crumbs are formed.
3. Pour into bowl, add apple cider and almond extract, and mix with fork until well blended and moist.
4. Press into bottom and sides of 8½-inch round pan. Set aside and prepare filling.
5. Add all filling ingredients to blender or food processor. Process until smooth and pour into prepared crust.
6. Bake at 375°F. until golden and slightly puffy. Allow to cool completely.
7. Meanwhile, prepare topping. Simmer apricots, covered, in ¾ cup apple cider with cinnamon and vanilla bean for 30 minutes. There should be very little liquid left. Allow to cool.

8. Remove vanilla bean.
9. Add apricot mixture to clean blender or food processor with ½ cup more apple cider. Process until smooth.
10. Dissolve kuzo in remaining cider. Pour into saucepan.
11. Add apricot purée and simmer, stirring constantly until smooth and glossy.
12. Pour over top of cooled pie to form glaze, and chill until it sets, before serving. It tastes great made a day in advance.

Serves 6–8

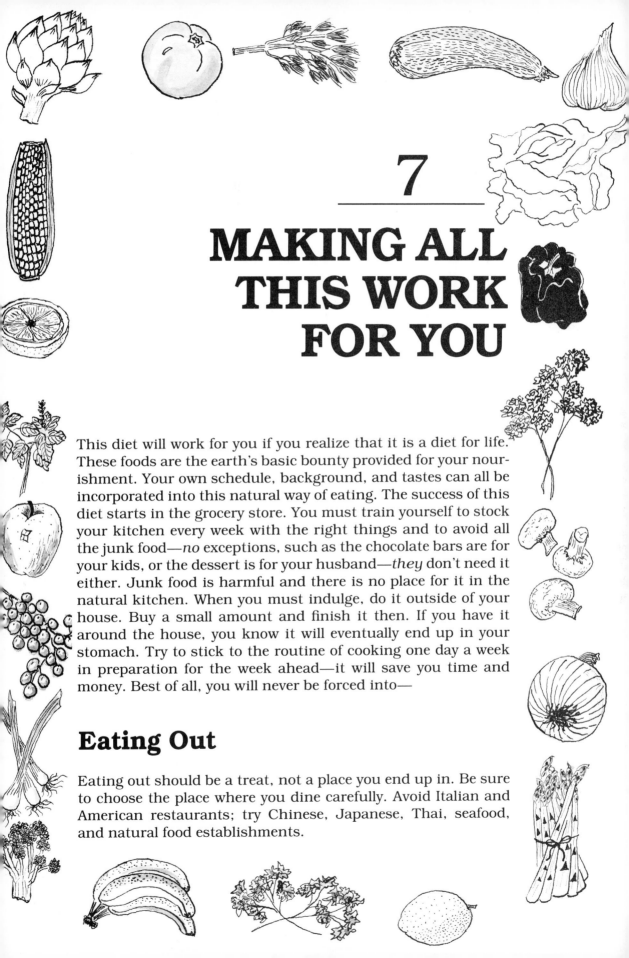

7

MAKING ALL THIS WORK FOR YOU

This diet will work for you if you realize that it is a diet for life. These foods are the earth's basic bounty provided for your nourishment. Your own schedule, background, and tastes can all be incorporated into this natural way of eating. The success of this diet starts in the grocery store. You must train yourself to stock your kitchen every week with the right things and to avoid all the junk food—*no* exceptions, such as the chocolate bars are for your kids, or the dessert is for your husband—*they* don't need it either. Junk food is harmful and there is no place for it in the natural kitchen. When you must indulge, do it outside of your house. Buy a small amount and finish it then. If you have it around the house, you know it will eventually end up in your stomach. Try to stick to the routine of cooking one day a week in preparation for the week ahead—it will save you time and money. Best of all, you will never be forced into—

Eating Out

Eating out should be a treat, not a place you end up in. Be sure to choose the place where you dine carefully. Avoid Italian and American restaurants; try Chinese, Japanese, Thai, seafood, and natural food establishments.

Guidelines for Dining Out

1. When you order, think of what you've already eaten that day. If you've had a lot of vegetables, order protein, such as poultry or seafood. If you've had protein, consider a big salad. Unfortunately, many restaurants do not serve grains and very few prepare vegetables well. Try to eat these things at home, and enjoy seafood or poultry in restaurants.
2. Ask for your food to be prepared without monosodium glutamate (MSG) or butter and order all sauces *on the side.*
3. Don't forget to consider the appetizer list. Very often the healthier fare is to be found there. Two appetizers can make a lovely dinner.
4. Eat what you want. Stop when you're full.
5. Forget the bread basket; don't even have it *near* you.
6. If you really want a dessert, order one and *share.* Enjoy a bite or two—savor the flavor—and ask for the check!
7. Alcohol is really fattening—try to avoid it. When you do indulge stick to light, not sweet, drinks—wine, light beer, and mineral water are best.
8. Try to dine early in the evening, at least two hours before retiring.
9. Enjoy the difference! When the others are pushing away from the table, disgusted with themselves, groaning about how full they are and how they have to start dieting tomorrow, you will feel great and know that you're already on your way!

8

FAT-FREE FOREVER!

Once you have completed the 30-Day Menu Plan, it's time for a re-evaluation. Weigh and remeasure your body. Take a good long look at your unclothed body in the mirror. If you still have a way to go, repeat the Thirty-Day Menu Plan, following it closely. If you are now your ideal weight, adapt your eating to these principles and loosen the structure.

Remember though that this diet is about more than weight loss. Think of how good this food makes you *feel* as well as look. The basic diet is one to be followed forever.

Each day be sure to have a grain, a protein, and plenty of fresh vegetables. Remember that the type of eating you do is a habit; try to keep the habit in the positive direction—nourishing, not punishing, yourself with food. Everything you take in shows— *give yourself the chance to be beautiful. . . .*

Best wishes always,

Annette Annechild

Annette Annechild

Index